DISTRICT OF COLUMBIA:
CURRENT ISSUES

DISTRICT OF COLUMBIA: CURRENT ISSUES

DOUGLAS H. MARTIN (EDITOR)

Novinka Books
New York

Senior Editors: Susan Boriotti and Donna Dennis
Coordinating Editor: Tatiana Shohov
Office Manager: Annette Hellinger
Graphics: Wanda Serrano
Editorial Production: Marius Andronie, Maya Columbus, Vladimir Klestov,
        Matthew Kozlowski, Tom Moceri and Anthony T. Sovak
Circulation: Ave Maria Gonzalez, Vera Popovic, Luis Aviles, Raymond Davis,
        Melissa Diaz, Magdalene Nunez, Marlene Nunez and Jeannie Pappas
Communications and Acquisitions: Serge P. Shohov
Marketing: Cathy DeGregory

Library of Congress Cataloging-in-Publication Data

District of Columbia: current issues / [edited by] Douglas H. Martin.
    p. cm.
    Includes index.
    ISBN 1-59033-707-7 (softcover)
    1. Washington (D.C.)—Politics and government—1995- 2. Washington (D.C.)—
Politics and government. I. Martin, Douglas H.

JK2716.D57 2003
320.9753—dc21

                                                                        2003010368

Copyright © 2003 by Novinka Books, An Imprint of
       Nova Science Publishers, Inc.
       400 Oser Ave, Suite 1600
       Hauppauge, New York 11788-3619
       Tele. 631-231-7269   Fax 631-231-8175
       e-mail: Novascience@earthlink.net
       Web Site: http://www.novapublishers.com

All rights reserved. No part of this book may be reproduced, stored in a retrieval system or transmitted in any form or by any means: electronic, electrostatic, magnetic, tape, mechanical photocopying, recording or otherwise without permission from the publishers.

The authors and publisher have taken care in preparation of this book, but make no expressed or implied warranty of any kind and assume no responsibility for any errors or omissions. No liability is assumed for incidental or consequential damages in connection with or arising out of information contained in this book.

This publication is designed to provide accurate and authoritative information with regard to the subject matter covered herein. It is sold with the clear understanding that the publisher is not engaged in rendering legal or any other professional services. If legal or any other expert assistance is required, the services of a competent person should be sought. FROM A DECLARATION OF PARTICIPANTS JOINTLY ADOPTED BY A COMMITTEE OF THE AMERICAN BAR ASSOCIATION AND A COMMITTEE OF PUBLISHERS.

Printed in the United States of America

CONTENTS

Preface		vii
Chapter 1	Background and History of the District of Columbia	1
Chapter 2	District of Columbia Delegates to Congress *Michael K. Fauntroy*	13
Chapter 3	District of Columbia Voting Representation in Congress: Background, Issues, and Options *Michael K. Fauntroy*	23
Chapter 4	District of Columbia: A Brief History of Congressional Actions Affecting the Board of Education *Eugene Boyd and Carol Glover*	43
Chapter 5	District of Columbia Tuition Assistance Program *Bonnie Mangan*	63
Chapter 6	District of Columbia Department of Corrections: Transfer of Functions to the Federal Government *JoAnne O'Bryant*	67
Chapter 7	District of Columbia Management Restoration Act of 1999: A Fact Sheet *Eugene Boyd*	89
Chapter 8	District of Columbia Appropriations Act for FY2003: Comparison of General Provisions of P.L. 107-96 and S. 2809 *Eugene Boyd*	93
Chapter 9	District of Columbia Terrorism Response *Eugene Boyd and Michael Fauntroy*	107
Index		111

PREFACE

The District of Columbia has long addressed issues pertaining to controversial governmental policies, congressional representation, etc. This outstanding book examines the background and current issues along with the problems that have been creating controversy for over 200 years.

Chapter 1

BACKGROUND AND HISTORY OF THE DISTRICT OF COLUMBIA[*]

When the United States Constitution was adopted on September 15, 1787, Article 1, Section 8, Clause 17, included language authorizing the establishment of a federal district. This district was not to exceed 10 miles square, under the exclusive legislative authority of Congress. On July 16, 1790, Congress authorized President George Washington to choose a permanent site for the capital city and, on December 1, 1800, the capital was moved from Philadelphia to an area along the Potomac River. The census of 1800 showed that the new capital had a population of 14,103.

The District of Columbia Bicentennial Commission was established to develop plans for the celebration of various anniversary dates in District of Columbia history. The commission is comprised of 39 members with a specified number of commissioners appointed by the mayor, the chairman of the D.C. Council, council members, the District delegate to the House of Representatives, the courts, and the District of Columbia Bar. Among the events celebrated are the 200th anniversary of the Residency Act, which established that there shall be a permanent seat of government on the Potomac River (July 16, 1990); the 200th anniversary of President George Washington's proclamation of the site for the federal district (January 24, 1991); and the 200th anniversary of the arrival of Pierre L'Enfant, Benjamin Banneker and Andrew Ellicott. The commission may designate other bicentennial events for celebration.

---

[*] Sources: Office of Public Records. Historical Society website: http://www.hswdc.org.

There have been several forms of appointed and elected governments in the District of Columbia: an appointed, three-member commission (1790-1802); elected councils and an appointed mayor (1802-1820); elected councils and an elected mayor (1820-1871); an appointed governor, a two-house legislature (one appointed and the other elected), and an elected, non-voting delegate to the Congress (1871-1874); and another appointed, three-member commission (1874-1967). Following the defeat by Congress of a home rule effort in 1967, then-President Lyndon B. Johnson reorganized the District government and created the positions of an appointed mayor/commissioner and an appointed nine-member council.

District residents won the right to vote in a presidential election on March 29, 1961, to elect a board of education in 1968 and, in 1970, to elect a non-voting delegate to the House of Representatives. In 1973, Congress approved a bill that provided District residents with an elected form of government with limited home rule authority; as a result, District residents voted for a mayor and a council for the first time in more than 100 years. District residents accepted the home rule charter by referendum vote in 1974. Congress delegated to the District government the authority, functions and powers of a state, with a very important exception: Congress retains control over the District's revenue and expenditures by annually reviewing the entire District government budget. In addition, Congress has repeatedly prohibited the District from imposing a non-resident income tax.

In 1980, District voters approved a statehood initiative by a majority of 60 percent; delegates to a statehood constitutional convention were elected in 1981 and, in 1983, a bill for the admission of the state of New Columbia was introduced in Congress. The "Constitution for the State of New Columbia" is still under congressional consideration and is reintroduced into each new congressional session. Under the specifications of the statehood initiatives, most of the land area of the District of Columbia would become the state of New Columbia; the District of Columbia would continue to exist, albeit reduced in size to an area consisting of the White House, the Capitol, the Supreme Court, the Mall and federal monuments and government buildings adjacent to the Mall.

WASHINGTON, D.C.

The US Congress met in a variety of cities - Philadelphia, New York, and Princeton (New Jersey) among them - before the fledgling republic was ready to commit to a permanent seat of government. Congress chose the Potomac as a natural midpoint that would satisfy both northern and southern states (whose cultural and political differences were apparent well before the Civil War of 1861-1865). This spot had the added benefit of being across the river from George Washington's home in Mount Vernon.

Folks started referring to it as 'the city of Washington' around 1791 and the name stuck. Maryland and Virginia agreed to cede land to create the District of Columbia (named for Christopher Columbus), and an area 'ten miles square' (26 sq km) was laid out by African American mathematician Benjamin Banneker and surveyor Andrew Ellicott. French engineer Pierre Charles L'Enfant was hired to design the city, and though his elegant plan was widely admired, he quickly ran afoul of local politics. After L'Enfant was fired, Banneker continued to carry out L'Enfant's plans.

Work started on the ornate Capitol in 1793, but it was barely complete when British troops torched it in the War of 1812. Though the Capitol was eventually rebuilt, the city entered a slump from which it wouldn't recover for decades. A dispirited vote to abandon the capital lost by only nine votes.

Charles Dickens visited and dismissed DC as 'the City of Magnificent Distances,' complaining about 'spacious avenues that begin in nothing and lead nowhere; streets, milelong, that only want houses, roads, and inhabitants; public buildings that need but a public.'

The Civil War focused attention on Washington, bringing bivouacs, temporary hospitals, and armies to its outskirts. The war's chaos and expense led Washingtonians to wonder whether construction of the elaborate Capitol dome might not be suspended. President Lincoln responded, 'If people see the Capitol going on, it is a sign we intend the Union shall go on.' In the war's aftermath, the Great Emancipator was assassinated in Ford's Theater (a memorial flag remains draped over the theater box shrine today), and the role of the US capital changed from state-led administration to centralized leadership.

The town's ailing infrastructure was overhauled in the 1870s by territorial governor Alexander 'Boss' Shepherd, whose extravagant use of federal funds and penchant for steamrolling anything in his way led to a crackdown by Congress that robbed DC of self-government for another 100 years. For the citizenry, it was a high price to pay for a city beginning to look like it might fulfill L'Enfant's original vision of a world-class capital.

A beautification plan at the turn of the century added most of the landscaping, parks, and monuments for which Washington is now well known. Nevertheless, until recently Washington suffered from its image as a

Southern backwater. It was John F Kennedy who so succinctly slammed it as 'a city of Southern efficiency and Northern charm.' The Kennedy Center, established as a 'living memorial' to JFK, did much to bring cosmopolitan culture to the place.

The city's intense and divisive political climate is downright *romantic* to political activists. Spectacular *free* art is visible at every turn. From a Southern backwater, DC has evolved into a national pilgrimage center for many citizens (as was intended). Yet Washington is notorious too for the many severe problems that trouble its residents. Poverty, crime, and racial segregation in the shadow of glorious monuments proclaiming 'equality for all' embarrass those who would hope to hold the nation's capital up as a model. Washington, DC, is no model, but it is a microcosm - of the grand ideals and grim realities of the USA.

On September 11, 2001, terrorists attacked Washington, flying a hijacked United Airlines aircraft into the Pentagon, causing significant damage and killing all aboard the plane. A further plane crash-landed near Shanksville, Pennsylvania, it too intended to hit a Washington target. The Washington attack was part of a systematic terrorist operation by the al Qaeda terrorist network, using hijacked aircraft as weapons. On the same day two hijacked planes destroyed New York's twin towers, killing thousands of people. The terrorist attacks were the worst-ever on US soil.

In 2003, despite security remaining high around Washington's key monuments, it is clear that the city has gone a long way towards repairing both the Pentagon and its damaged psyche, with visitors returning and hotels refilling. And, while crime remains a problem and District finances still need help, Washington's city is once more a place to live, not just to visit.

FREQUENTLY ASKED QUESTIONS ABOUT WASHINGTON, D.C.

Why is Washington, D.C. our nation's capital?
Between 1776 and 1800, Congress met in several different locations. Philadelphia served as the last temporary capital from 1790-1800. The location of the permanent seat of the federal government was a controversial issue that divided Americans for many years. Various possibilities were suggested and many compromises were made until finally on July 16, 1790, Congress passed a law that permitted President George Washington to select

a location for the national capital along the Potomac River and to appoint three commissioners to oversee its development. Washington selected a ten square mile area of land from property in Maryland and Virginia that lay on both sides of the Potomac. (In 1846, land formerly belonging to Virginia was returned to that state.) Congress met for the first time in the new capital on November 21, 1800 and the transfer of the government from Philadelphia was completed by June of 1801.

How did the city get its name?

Shortly after the owners of the land selected for the capital transferred their property to the government, President Washington began to refer to the newly-created town as "the Federal City." At a meeting on September 9, 1791, the commissioners agreed that the "Federal district shall be called the 'Territory of Columbia' and the Federal City the 'City of Washington.'" (The term "district" was more popularly used than "territory" and officially replaced it when the capital was incorporated in 1871.) The name "Washington" was chosen by the commissioners to honor the President. "Columbia," a feminine form of "Columbus," was popularized as a name for America in patriotic poetry and song after the Revolutionary War. The term idealized America's qualities as a land of liberty.

What design is on Washington, D.C.'s flag?

The design for the flag of the District of Columbia was approved in 1938. It consists of three red stars above two horizontal red stripes on a white field. The design was taken from the shield on the coat of arms of George Washington's family, which appeared on one of the earliest maps of the district in 1792.

How is D.C. different than a state?

Like other citizens living in states, D.C. citizens pay full federal and local taxes, but they do not get the privileges of representation and independence that the states have. Also, unlike the states, when D.C. receives federal funding, the funding comes with directives on how the money should be spent. D.C. residents do not have voting representatives in the Senate or in the House of Representatives to protect their interests. They have nonvoting representation that can sit on committees, but the representatives cannot vote on bills affecting their District. Senators and members of Congress from the states have voting powers. D.C. residents have a limited Presidential vote equal to the smallest state regardless of their population, and have only had the right to vote for the President since the 1964 election. Unlike states who can appoint their own local judges, the President appoints D.C.'s local judges. Congress only delegated power to a locally elected mayor and 13-member city council in 1974, and Congress continues to review and modify D.C.'s laws and budget. No states have their laws and budget reviewed or appointed mayors and city councils.

Why is D.C. no longer 10 square miles?

In 1846, the area encompassed by the city of Alexandria and Alexandria County (now Arlington County), was retroceded to Virginia. As a result of this process, the federal district lost one third of its total area. Merchants in Alexandria had expected to gain commercial benefits from being associated with the national capital, but the city quickly stagnated with disputes over the canal and competition with the port of Georgetown. Merchants and traders who expected to become rich were disappointed, because the federal government had no need for the land south of the Potomac River. As part of the District, they had not only lost the right to vote and representation but also potential economic growth. The slave trade was a third, though unstated, reason for the retrocession. The slave trade flourished in Alexandria and by removing the city from congressional authority, Alexandria was able to keep its active business until slavery was outlawed. Also retrocession gave Virginia's slaveholders two additional representatives in Virginia. Alexandria's voters petitioned Congress asking for the return of the land to Virginia, but it wasn't until they petitioned the Virginia legislature in 1846 that they were able to retrocede.

CHRONOLOGY OF SOME EVENTS IN THE HISTORY OF THE DISTRICT OF COLUMBIA

May 15, 1751: The Maryland Assembly appoints commissioners to lay a town on the Potomac River, above the mouth of Rock Creek, on 60 acres of land to be purchased from George Gordon and George Beall. This settlement becomes Georgetown.

February 27, 1752: The survey and plat of Georgetown into 80 lots is completed.

September 17, 1787: The Constitution is signed by the members of the Constitutional Convention.

June 21, 1788: The 1788 U.S. Constitution, as adopted by the Constitutional Convention on September 15, 1787, is ratified by the states. Article 1, Section 8, Clause 17, gives Congress authority "to exercise exclusive legislation in all cases whatsoever, over such District (not exceeding ten miles square) as may by cession of particular States, and the acceptance of Congress, become the seat of the government of the United States...."

July 16, 1790: The Residency Act of 1790 gives the president power to choose a site for the capital city on the east bank of the Potomac River between the mouth of the Eastern Branch and the Connogocheague Creek (now Conococheague) near Hagerstown, nearly 70 miles upstream.

January 22, 1791: George Washington appoints Thomas Johnson and Daniel Carroll of Rock Creek, representing Maryland and Dr. David Stuart, to represent Virginia, as "Commissioners for surveying the District of (sic) Territory accepted by the said Act for the permanent seat of the Government of the United States...."

January 24, 1791: President George Washington selects a site that includes portions of Maryland and Virginia.

December 1, 1800: The federal capital is transferred from Philadelphia to the site on the Potomac River now called the City of Washington, in the territory of Columbia. At the time of the 1800 census, the population of the new capital included 10,066 whites, 793 free Negroes and 3,244 slaves.

February 27, 1801: Congress divides the [District] into the counties of Washington and Alexandria.

May 3, 1802: Congress grants the City of Washington its first municipal charter. Voters, defined as white males who pay taxes and have lived in the city for at least a year, receive the right to elect a 12-member council. The mayor is appointed by the president.

May 4, 1812: Congress amends the charter of the City of Washington to provide for an eight-member board of aldermen and a 12-member common council. The aldermen and the common council elect the mayor.

March 15, 1820: Under the Act of 1820, Congress amends the Charter of the City of Washington for the direct election of the mayor by resident voters.

July 9, 1846: Congress passes a law returning the city of Alexandria and Alexandria County to the state of Virginia.

May 17, 1848: Congress adopts a new charter for the City of Washington and expands the number of elected offices to include a board of assessors, a surveyor, a collector and a registrar.

April 16, 1862: Congress abolishes slavery in the federal district (the City of Washington, Washington County, and Georgetown). This action predates both the Emancipation Proclamation and the adoption of the 13th Amendment to the Constitution.

January 8, 1867: Congress grants black males the right to vote in local elections.

June 1, 1871: The elected mayor and council of Washington City and Georgetown, and the County Levy Court are abolished by Congress and replaced by a governor and council appointed by the president. An elected House of Delegates and a non-voting delegate to Congress are created. In this act, the jurisdiction and territorial government came to be called the District of Columbia, thus combining the governments of Georgetown, the City of Washington and the County of Washington. A seal and motto, "Justitia Omnibus" (Justice for All), are adopted for the District of Columbia.

June 20, 1874: The territorial government of the District of Columbia, including the non-voting delegate to Congress, is abolished. Three temporary commissioners and a subordinate military engineer are appointed by the president.

June 11, 1878: In The Organic Act of 1878, Congress approves the establishment of the District of Columbia government as a municipal corporation governed by three presidentially appointed commissioners - two civilian commissioners and a commissioner from the military corps of engineers. This form of government lasted until August 1967.

July 4, 1906: The District Building, on 14th Street and Pennsylvania Avenue, becomes the official City Hall.

July 1, 1952: The Reorganization Plan of 1952 transfers to the three commissioners the functions of more than 50 boards.

March 29, 1961: The 23rd Amendment to the Constitution gives District residents the right to vote for president.

February 20, 1967: The Washington Metropolitan Area Transit Authority is created through a compact between the District of Columbia, Maryland and Virginia.

April 22, 1968: District residents receive the right to elect a Board of Education.

December 24, 1973: Congress approves the District of Columbia Self-Government and Governmental Reorganization Act, P.L. 93-198, which establishes an elected mayor and a 13-member council.

May 7, 1974: Voters of the District of Columbia approve by referendum the District Charter and the establishment of advisory neighborhood commissions. General elections are held for mayor and council on November 5, 1974.

January 2, 1975: The newly elected Mayor Walter Washington and first elected council take office.

February 3, 1976: The first election for advisory neighborhood commissioners is held.

March 29, 1978: The first segment of the Metrorail Red Line opens.

August 22, 1978: Congress approves the District of Columbia Voting Rights Amendment, which would give District residents voting representation in the House and the Senate. The proposed constitutional amendment was not ratified by the necessary number of states (38) within the allotted seven years.

January 2, 1979: The Mayor Marion Barry takes office.

November 4, 1980: District electors approve the District of Columbia Statehood Constitutional Convention of 1979, which became D.C. Law 3-171 and which called for convening a state constitutional convention.

November 2, 1982: After the constitutional convention, a Constitution for the State of New Columbia is ratified by District voters.

October 1, 1984: The District enters the municipal bond market.

October 29, 1986: Congress approves an amendment to the District of Columbia Stadium Act of 1957, which authorizes the transfer of Robert F. Kennedy Stadium from the federal government to the District of Columbia government.

February 20, 1987: The Metropolitan Washington Airports Authority is created to acquire Washington National and Washington - Dulles International airports from the federal government, pursuant to P.L. 99-151, The Metropolitan Washington Airports Act of 1986. The authority begins operating the airports on June 7, 1987.

October 1, 1987: Saint Elizabeth's Hospital is transferred to the District of Columbia government pursuant to P.L. 98-621, The St. Elizabeth's Hospital and the D.C. Mental Health Services Act of 1984.

January 2, 1992: Mayor Sharon Pratt Dixon, the first woman mayor, takes office.

January 2, 1995: Marion Barry takes office for an unprecedented fourth term as Mayor of the District of Columbia.

April 17, 1995: President Clinton signed the law creating a presidentially appointed District of Columbia Financial Control Board and a mayor-appointed Chief Financial Officer.

July 13, 1995: The newly appointed financial control board holds its first public meeting. It is composed of Dr. Andrew Brimmer, chair; and members: Joyce A. Ladner, Constance B. Newman, Stephen D. Harlan and Edward A. Singletary. John Hill is the Executive Director and Daniel Rezneck is the General Counsel.

February 14, 1996: Mayor Barry announces a transformation plan to reduce the size of government and increase its efficiency.

DC STATISTICS

Population	572,059
Male	269,366 (47.1%)
Female	302,693 (52.9%)
Black	343,312 (60.0%)
White	176,101 (30.8%)
Asian	15,189 (2.7%)
American Indian and Alaska Native	1,713 (0.3%)
Other race	21,950 (3.8%)
Two or more races	13,446 (2.4%)
Hispanic/Latino	44,953 (7.9%)
Percentage of population 18 and over	79.9%
65 and over	12.3%
Median age	34.6

FACTS ABOUT D.C.

Capital	It is the capital of the United States.
Mayor	Anthony Williams (to January 2003) (D).
Entered the Union	February 21, 1871 (as a municipal corporation)
Motto	Justitia omnibus (Justice to all)
Flower	American Beauty rose
Tree	Scarlet Oak
Bird	Wood Thrush
Sports Teams	DC Freedom (Women's Soccer); DC United (Men's Soccer); Washington Capitals (Hockey); Washington Mystics (Women's Basketball); Washington Redskins (Football); Washington Wizards (Men's Basketball)
Origin of Name	The district is named after Christopher Columbus
Major Industries	Federal government, tourism
Land Area	68.25 square miles (177 square kilometers)
Altitude	Highest, 420 ft.; lowest, sea level
Average Daily Temperature	Jan., 35.2 degrees F; July, 78.9 degrees F

Chapter 2

DISTRICT OF COLUMBIA DELEGATES TO CONGRESS

Michael K. Fauntroy

ABSTRACT

District of Columbia voting rights and representation in Congress is an issue of perennial concern, as it raises the question of how to balance constitutional dictates and representative democracy. The office of Delegate to Congress has existed since 1787. The District of Columbia has had elected Delegates during two periods from 1871 to 1875, and since 1971. The role of Delegates was the subject of considerable debate at one point because the Constitution is silent on the position. The District of Columbia Delegate Act of 1970 established the current position of D.C. Delegate. Since passage of the Act, District residents have elected two individuals to serve in Congress.

BACKGROUND, 1787-1970: WHAT IS A DELEGATE TO CONGRESS?

The position of Delegate to Congress, which predates the Constitution, was created when the Congress of the Confederation enacted what has come to be known as the Northwest Ordinance of 1787. The ordinance established what Congress anticipated would be a temporary territorial government; and it created and authorized the territorial legislature "to elect a delegate to Congress, who shall have a seat in Congress, with a right of debating, but not of voting, during this temporary government."[1] The United States Constitution itself, however, is silent on the matter, but upon ratification of the Constitution, Congress gave full statutory effect to the Northwest Ordinance through reenactment in 1789.

The newly reenacted Ordinance was slightly modified to adapt to the Constitution and to allow for the popular election of a territorial house of representatives who, along with an appointed legislative council, would elect a Delegate to Congress. While the Ordinance clearly stated that the Delegate could not vote – though it did not distinguish between voting on the floor and committees – it was silent on the full nature of the Delegate's duties, privileges, and obligations. This silence arguably leaves the Delegate's role open to interpretation, which was further complicated because the Constitution allows each House to determine the rules of its proceedings.[2]

Committee service was one area in which Delegate participation was unclear.[3] Beginning in 1795, Delegates were members of select committees and conference committees. By 1841, Delegates' roles in the House were becoming institutionalized:

> With the single exception of voting, the Delegate enjoys every other privilege and exercises every other right of a Representative. He can act as a member of a standing or special committee and vote on the business before said committees, and he may thus exercise an important influence on those initiatory proceedings by which business is prepared for the action of

---

[1] U.S. Congress of the Confederation, An Ordinance for the government of the territory of the United States northwest of the river Ohio, July 13, 1787. In U.S. Congress, *The Federal and State Constitutions, Colonial Charters, and Other Organic Laws of the States, Territories, and Colonies Now or Heretofore Forming the United States of America*, Francis Newton Thorpe, ed. 59th Cong., 2d sess., House Document 59-357 (Washington: GPO, 1909), vol. 2, p.960. Earlier ordinances provided for territorial representation in Congress, but they were never put into effect. See, for example, an ordinance of 1784 discussed in Julian Boyd, ed., *The Papers of Thomas Jefferson*, vol. 6, (Princeton, NJ: Princeton University Press, 1952), pp. 613-615. Earlier proposals are discussed in Archer Butler Hulbert, ed., *Ohio in the Time of the Confederation* (Marietta, OH: Marietta Historical Commission, 1918). pp. 1-12.

[2] U.S. Constitution, Article 1, Section 5, Clause 2.

[3] For a detailed discussion on committee service for Delegates to Congress, see *Territorial Delegates to the U.S. Congress: A Brief History*, by Andorra Bruno, CRS Report 97-143 GOV (Washington: Jan. 23, 1997), 11 pp.; and Jo Tice Bloom, "Early Delegates in the House of Representatives," in John Porter Bloom, ed., *The American Territorial System* (Athens, OH: Ohio University Press, 1973), pp. 65-76.

the House. He is also required to take an oath to support the Constitution of the United States.[4]

Toward the close of the 19th Century, Delegates become more integrated into the congressional system. Assignment of Delegates to standing committees occurred in 1871 under a House rule which called for a Delegate to serve on the Committee on the Territories and the D.C. Delegate to serve on the Committee for the District of Columbia. Additional committee assignments were authorized in 1876, 1880, and 1887.[5]

Until 1970, Delegates generally represented territories on their way to statehood. An exception is the District of Columbia, which elected a Delegate to Congress who served from 1871[6] to 1874.[7] In 1970, however, Congress began authorizing Delegates from areas for which statehood did not appear to be imminent: From the District of Columbia in 1970;[8] from the U.S. Virgin Islands and Guam in 1972;[9] and from American Samoa in 1978.[10] Puerto Rico has been represented in Congress by a Resident Commissioner since 1902, and the Philippines were represented in Congress by a Resident Commissioner until independence in 1946. The Northern Marianas Islands, also a U.S. Territory, is not represented in Congress.

DISTRICT OF COLUMBIA DELEGATE TO CONGRESS

The District of Columbia Delegate Act of 1970 gave District residents the right to elect one person to represent them in the House of Representatives:

---

[4] U.S. Congress, House of Representatives, H.Rept 10, 27th Cong., 1st Sess. Quoted in Asher C. Hinds, *Hinds' Precedents of the House of Representatives of the United States* (Washington: GPO, 1907), vol. 2, Sec. 1301, p. 865.
[5] *Hinds' Precedents*, vol. 2, Sec. 1297, p. 864.
[6] 16 Stat. 419.
[7] 18 Stat. 116. In 1874, Congress eliminated the locally elected District government and with it the position of Delegate to Congress. Norton P. Chipman served as delegate from April 21, 1871, until the close of the 43rd Congress on March 3, 1875. During his tenure, he sat on the House Committee on the District of Columbia.
[8] P.L. 91-405, 84 Stat. 845. The House bill H.R. 18725, 91st Cong. (H.Rept. 91-1385), passed the House on Aug. 10, 1970. The Senate passed H.R. 18725 (S.Rept. 91-1122) on Sept. 9, 1970. It was signed into law on Sept. 22, 1970.
[9] P.L. 92-271; 86 Stat. 118.
[10] P.L. 95-556; 92 Stat. 2078.

The Delegate shall have a seat in the House of Representatives, with the right of debate, but not of voting, shall have all the privileges granted a Representative by section 6 of Article 1 of the Constitution, and shall be subject to the same restrictions and regulations as are imposed by law or rules on Representatives. The Delegate shall be elected to serve during each Congress.[11]

Thus, the rights and prerogatives of the District's Delegate in parliamentary matters are like those of other Delegates. Former House Parliamentarian Wm. Holmes Brown describes the role of Delegates in practice as follows:

Sec. 1. In General
   The Delegates and Resident Commissioners are those statutory officers who represent in the House the constituencies of territories and properties owned or administered by the United States but not admitted to statehood (Deschler Ch. 7 Sec. 3). The Virgin Islands, Guam, and American Samoa, as well as the District of Columbia, are represented in the House by a Delegate, while Puerto Rico is represented by a Resident Commissioner (Manual Sec. 740). The rights and prerogatives of a Delegate in parliamentary matters are not limited to legislation affecting his own territory (6 Cannon Sec. 240).

Sec. 2. In the House
   The floor privileges of a Delegate or a Resident Commissioner in the House include the right to debate (2 Hinds Sec. 1290), make motions (2 Hinds Sec. 1291), and raise points of order (6 Cannon Sec. 240); but he cannot vote in the House nor serve as its presiding officer. See Manual Sec. 740. He may make any motion a Member may make (2 Hinds Sec. 1292) including the motion to adjourn (97-1, Jan. 9, 1981, p. 248), but not the motion to reconsider (2 Hinds Sec. 1292), which is itself dependent on the right to vote. He may make reports for committees (Manual Sec. 740) and may object to the consideration of a bill (6 Cannon Sec. 241; Deschler Ch. 7 Sec. 3.7). Impeachment proceedings have been moved by a Delegate (2 Hinds Sec. 1303.).

Sec. 3. In Committees
   The House rules now extend to Delegates and the Resident Commissioner all the powers in committee held by constitutional Members of the House. They are elected to serve on standing committees in the same manner as Members of the House and possess

---

[11] P.L. 91-405, Sec. 202; 84 Stat. 845.

in such committees the same powers and privileges as the other Members (Rule XII. Manual Sec. 740). They have the right to vote in committees on which they serve. Seniority accrual rights on committees have also been extended to the Delegates and Resident Commissioner (Deschler Ch. 7 Sec. 3.11). They may be appointed by the Speaker to any conference committee. The Speaker also now has the authority to appoint them to any select committee (Manual Sec. 701g), an appointment that previously required the permission of the House (94-2, Sept. 21, 1976, p. 31673).

Sec. 4. In Committee of the Whole

Under a rule adopted in 1993, when the House was sitting in Committee of the Whole, the Delegates and Resident Commissioner had the same powers and privileges as Members. In the same year, the Speaker was given authority to appoint a Delegate or Resident Commissioner as Chairman of the Committee of the Whole. These provisions were stricken from the rules as adopted in January 1995 (104-1, H. Res. 6).[12]

At the start of the 103rd Congress, the House approved a number of rules changes, including a controversial move to allow Delegates to vote in the Committee of the Whole. The rules change was proposed by District Delegate Norton who argued:

[There is no] constitutional barrier to extending the vote in the Committee of the Whole to all the House delegates. Article 1, Section 5, Clause 2 provides that "Each House may determine the Rules of its Proceedings." House rules have long interpreted this clause to permit delegates to vote in standing committees. Like the standing committees, the Committee of the Whole, into which the full House resolves itself, is a creature of the House rule-making power. Both are organizational expedients, nowhere mentioned in the Constitution, that are used to facilitate the legislative process. Voting by delegates in committees – whether subject-matter panels, such as Armed Services or Judiciary, or the largest of all, the Committee of the Whole – is permissible because committees do not pass final legislation and their actions are not binding on the House of Representatives.[13]

---

[12] Wm. Holmes Brown, *House Practice,* 104th Congress, 2nd Session (Washington: GPO, 1996), pp. 431, 432 [http://frwebgate.access.gpo.gov/cgi-bin/getdoc.cgi?dbname=104_house_practice&docid=hp-18], visited Mar. 26, 2001].

[13] Eleanor Holmes Norton, "Law, Politics, and Voting by Delegates: Bringing Democracy to the House," *Legal Times,* Jan. 4, 1993, pp. 22-23.

A lawsuit challenged the constitutionality to the amendment to Rule XII.[14] The claim of unconstitutionality was on the ground that "these rules unconstitutionally vest the Delegates with legislative power, and that they dilute the legislative power of Members of the House."[15] Ultimately, the provision allowing Delegate voting was upheld, provided that an immediate and automatic second ballot would occur in cases where Delegate votes provided the margin of victory on a particular question. Delegates would be prohibited from participating in the second ballot.

The rule change was reversed at the start of the 104th Congress.

Since passage of the District of Columbia Delegate Act in 1970, the District has elected two Delegates. The Rev. Dr. Walter E. Fauntroy was elected Delegate to Congress from the District on March 23, 1971, and took his seat in the 92nd Congress on April 19, 1971. Delegate Fauntroy served in the House of Representatives through the 101st Congress.[16] He served on the House Committee on the District of Columbia, where he chaired the Subcommittee on Fiscal Affairs and Health. He also served on the Committee on Banking, Finance and Urban Affairs where, for six years, he chaired the Subcommittee on International Development, Finance, Trade and Monetary Policy. At the time of his retirement from the House, Delegate Fauntroy was the third-ranking Democrat on the House Committee on Banking, Finance, and Urban Affairs.

Eleanor Holmes Norton succeeded Dr. Fauntroy as Delegate and has served in the House since the start of the 102nd Congress. Delegate Norton currently serves on the Committee on Government Reform, where she is the ranking Democrat on the Subcommittee on the District of Columbia, and also serves on the Subcommittee on Civil Service and Agency Organization. Delegate Norton is a member of the House Committee on Transportation and Infrastructure, where she serves on two subcommittees: Aviation; and Economic Development, Public Buildings, Hazardous Materials and Pipeline Transportation.

---

[14] *Michel v. Anderson*, No. 93-0039.
[15] 817 F. Supp. 126, at 2.
[16] Del. Fauntroy did not seek reelection to the 102nd Congress.

DISTRICT OF COLUMBIA REPRESENTATION IN CONGRESS: LEGISLATION

Legislation regarding District of Columbia representation in Congress has come, primarily, in four forms: bills to grant statehood to the District; bills to retrocede the District to the state of Maryland; bills calling for District residents to vote in Maryland for their representatives to the Senate and House; and bills seeking voting representation in the House proportional to the District's population.[17]

Statehood

Since the 98th Congress, 13 statehood bills have been introduced.[18] On two occasions, the bills were reported out of the committee of jurisdiction, resulting in one floor vote. The first of these two bills was introduced by Delegate Walter E. Fauntroy in 1987 to create a state that would have encompassed only the non-federal land in the District of Columbia.[19] While the bill was reported out of the House District Committee, no vote was taken on the House floor. On the second such statehood bill, introduced by Delegate Eleanor Holmes Norton in 1993, a vote was held that year, and the House voted 277-153 against passage.

---

[17] For a detailed discussion of local governance of the District of Columbia, see *Governance of the District of Columbia: A Brief History*, by Michael K. Fauntroy, CRS Report RL30897.

[18] In the 98th Congress, Del. Fauntroy introduced H.R. 3861 on Sept. 12, 1983 and, Sen. Kennedy introduced S. 2672 on May 15, 1984. In the 99th Congress, Fauntroy introduced H.R. 325 on Jan. 3, 1985; Kennedy introduced S. 293 on Jan. 24, 1985. In the 100th Congress, Fauntroy introduced H.R. 51 on Jan. 6, 1987; Kennedy introduced S. 863 on Mar. 26, 1987. In the 101st Congress, Fauntroy introduced H.R. 51 on Jan. 3, 1989; Kennedy introduced S. 2647 on May 17, 1990. In the 102nd Congress, Del. Norton introduced H.R. 2482 on May 29, 1991; Kennedy introduced S. 2023 on Nov. 22, 1991. In the 103rd Congress, Norton introduced H.R. 51 on Jan. 5, 1993.

[19] Del. Fauntroy introduced H.R. 51 on Jan. 6, 1987. On Sept. 17, 1987, the bill was reported to House, with amendments, by House Committee on District of Columbia, Report No: 100-305 and placed on Union Calendar No. 188.

Retrocession

Since the 101st Congress, there have been six bills that would retrocede the District to the state of Maryland.[20] The bills would maintain exclusive legislative authority and control of Congress over the National Capital Service Area in the District of Columbia. There have been no hearings or votes on these bills.

District Residents Voting in Maryland

Since the 101st Congress, one bill has been introduced to allow District residents to vote in federal elections as Maryland residents: H.R. 4193, introduced by Representative Stan Parris on March 6, 1990. The bill would have allowed, for the purposes of representation in the Congress and election of the President and Vice President, the right of the people of the District of Columbia to be treated as residents of the State of Maryland and to be eligible to participate in federal elections as Maryland residents, in accordance with the laws of the State of Maryland. The bill would have allowed residents of the District of Columbia to have one Representative in the House of Representatives and have their vote counted in the election of the two Senators from Maryland. Further, for purposes of determining eligibility to serve as a member of the House of Representatives or the Senate, a resident of the District of Columbia would have been considered an inhabitant of the State of Maryland. No hearings were held on the bill.

Voting Representation in Congress

Bills in this category sought votes on the House floor for the District's Delegate, two Senators, and proportional representation in the House for the District, or some variation thereof. On July 14, 1998, Delegate Eleanor Holmes Norton introduced H.R.4208 (105th Congress), a bill to provide for full voting representation in the Congress for the District of Columbia. On

---

[20] In the 101st Congress, Rep. Regula introduced H.R. 4195 on Mar. 6, 1990. In the 102nd Congress, Regula introduced H.R. 1204 on Feb. 28, 1991. In the 103rd Congress, Regula introduced H.R. 1205 on Mar. 3, 1993. In the 104th Congress, Regula introduced H.R. 1028 on Feb. 23, 1995. In the 105th Congress, Regula introduced H.R. 831 on Feb. 25, 1997. In the 106th Congress, Regula introduced H.R. 558 on Feb. 3, 1999.

June 9, 1998, Norton introduced H. Res.464 (105th Congress), which sought to amend House rules and provide a vote in the Committee of the Whole to the Delegate to the House from the District of Columbia.[21] None of the bills passed.

---

[21] At the start of the 103rd Congress, House rules were amended allowing Delegates from the District of Columbia and Territories of the U.S. Virgin Islands, Guam, American Samoa, and the Resident Commissioner from Puerto Rico to vote on the House floor. The rule change was repealed at the start of the 104th Congress.

Chapter 3

DISTRICT OF COLUMBIA VOTING REPRESENTATION IN CONGRESS: BACKGROUND, ISSUES, AND OPTIONS

Michael K. Fauntroy

ABSTRACT

Full congressional representation for District of Columbia residents is a perennial issue that raises the question of how constitutional dictates on the political status of the District of Columbia are to be balanced with the principles of representative democracy. Article 1, Section 8, Clause 17 of the U.S. Constitution confers upon Congress responsibility for governing the seat of the federal government. Conversely, among the principles on which the United States was founded is that of governance with the consent of the governed, i.e., participation of the citizenry in the governing process. The District of Columbia is represented in Congress by a Delegate in the House of Representatives; it is not represented in the Senate. Like other Delegates and the Resident Commissioner from Puerto Rico, the Delegate to Congress from the District of Columbia is allowed to vote in committee, but not in either the House sitting as the Committee of the Whole or the House sitting as the House. The Delegate is allowed to accrue seniority, introduce and debate legislation, and chair committees and subcommittees. Further, the Delegate is subject to all House rules regarding conduct of Members.

Numerous legislative attempts have been made to allow the District's residents to elect full-voting representatives in the House and Senate. These legislative attempts have come, primarily, in four forms:

- Bills seeking voting representation in Congress,
- Bills to grant statehood to the District,
- Bills to retrocede the District to the State of Maryland, and
- Bills calling for District residents to vote in Maryland for their representatives to the House and Senate.

These options are discussed in this chapter, including arguments for and against each option. A review of legislation for each option is provided. The most recent attempt to grant the District voting representation in Congress is the "No Taxation without Representation Act of 2001," which would exempt District residents from federal individual income taxation until the District had congressional representation with voting rights equal to those of citizens of the states.

BACKGROUND

Residents of the District of Columbia, which was established in 1790,[22] have never had more than limited representation in Congress. The District has never had any directly elected representation in the Senate, and has been represented by a nonvoting Delegate in the House of Representatives for 33 years of its 214-year existence.[23] The District of Columbia Delegate Act of 1970 gave District residents the right to elect one person to represent them in the House of Representatives.[24] Like other Delegates and the Resident Commissioner from Puerto Rico, the Delegate may vote in committee, but not in either the House sitting as the Committee of the Whole or in the House sitting as the House.[25] The Delegate is allowed to accrue seniority,

---

[22] 1 Stat. 130.
[23] District of Columbia Delegates to the House of Representatives were: Norton P. Chipman (1871-1874), Walter E. Fauntroy (1971-1991), and Eleanor Holmes Norton (since 1991). For a detailed discussion of District of Columbia Delegates, see CRS Report RS20875, *District of Columbia Delegates to Congress,* by Michael K. Fauntroy.
[24] P.L. 91-405. While District residents were, in 1970, authorized to elect a Delegate to Congress, the 23rd Amendment, ratified in 1961, granted the District the right to appoint three electors for the purpose of electing the President and the Vice President.
[25] There was a two-year period in which Delegates and the Resident Commissioner from Puerto Rico could vote in the Committee of the Whole. At the start of the 103rd Congress, the House passed H.Res. 5, which amended House Rule XII to allow Delegates to vote in the Committee of the Whole: "In the Committee of the Whole House on the state of the Union,

introduce and debate legislation, and chair committees and subcommittees. Further, the Delegate is subject to all House rules regarding conduct of Members.

Full congressional representation for District of Columbia residents is a perennial issue that raises the question of how constitutional dictates on the political status of the District of Columbia are to be balanced with the principles of representative democracy. Article 1, Section 8, Clause 17 of the U.S. Constitution confers upon Congress responsibility for governing the seat of the federal government. Conversely, among the principles in which the United States was founded is that of governance with the consent of the governed, i.e., participation of the citizenry in the governing process.

In the wake of the District government's fiscal crisis during the mid-1990s, discussion of increased voting representation in Congress temporarily receded.[26] During those years Congress created the District of Columbia Financial Responsibility and Management Assistance Authority, popularly known as the Control Board, to overcome the crisis; and District residents elected a new mayor and some new members of the city council. With subsequent governmental and budgetary improvements and the termination of the Control Board at the end of fiscal year 2001, there is renewed interest in the question of full congressional voting representation for residents of the District of Columbia.

The current debate is notable for the increasingly visible slogan, "No taxation without representation," a slogan that recalls a Colonial-era grievance against the British Crown. An increasing number of District residents are arguing that, if they are treated like residents of United States territories who do not have full voting representation in Congress, then they, like territorial residents, should not be subject to federal income taxation.

---

the Resident Commissioner to the United States from Puerto Rico and each Delegate to the House shall possess the same powers and privileges as Members of the House." At the outset of the 104th Congress, however, H.Res. 6 amended House rules to deny Delegates and the Puerto Rican Resident Commissioner a vote in the Committee of the Whole. In the 105th Congress, D.C. Delegate Norton introduced H.Res. 464 to restore the right to vote in the Committee of the Whole, which was referred to the Committee on Rules, but no action was taken on the measure. For a detailed discussion on committee service for Delegates to Congress, see CRS Report 97-143 GOV, *Territorial Delegates to the U.S. Congress: A Brief History*, by Andorra Bruno; and Jo Tice Bloom, "Early Delegates in the House of Representatives," in *The American Territorial System*, John Porter Bloom, ed. (Athens, OH: Ohio University Press, 1973), pp. 65-76.

[26] For a detailed discussion of the evolution of local governance of the District of Columbia, see CRS Report RL3 0897, *Governance of the District of Columbia: A Brief History*, by Michael K. Fauntroy.

Companion bills H.R. 1193 and S. 603, the "No Taxation Without Representation Act of 2001," reflect that sentiment.[27] The bills call for full congressional representation for District residents and for exemption from federal individual income taxation until full congressional representation is provided.

LEGISLATIVE OPTIONS FOR D.C. CONGRESSIONAL REPRESENTATION

Legislative options regarding District of Columbia representation in Congress can be placed in four categories: (1) bills seeking full voting representation in Congress;[28] (7) bills granting statehood to the non-federal portion of the District; (3) bills retroceding the non-federal portion of the District to the State of Maryland; and (4) bills allowing District residents to vote in Maryland for their representatives to the Senate and House.[29]

Option 1: Voting Representation in Congress Equivalent to That of States

Legislation embodying this option would treat the District as if it were a state: the District would have two Senators and one or more Representatives in proportion to its population, with a minimum of one Representative. Article 1, Section 2 of the Constitution provides at least one Representative to each state. Congress has adopted a formula to allocate seats in the House among the states based on population.[30]

---

[27] Delegate Norton introduced H.R. 1193 on March 22, 2001. Senator Lieberman introduced the bill as S. 603 on March 23, 2001.
[28] Additional options that increase District voting representation in Congress but fall short of proportional representation in the House and two Senators are discussed at the end of this chapter.
[29] There are additional options that do not enhance District representation in Congress. One would be to maintain the status quo, with one non-voting Delegate in the House and no representation in the Senate. Another option would be to rescind the Delegate position. No legislation has been introduced that would abolish the Delegate position since its return in 1971.
[30] The size of the House of Representatives is fixed by law at 435 Members. Consequently, if this option were to be implemented, one of the following steps would have to be taken: (a) the size of the House of Representatives would have to be permanently increased, or (b) it could be temporarily increased until the next decennial census reallocates seats to the states,

Congress pursued this option through the constitutional amendment process. In March 1967, President Lyndon Johnson forwarded to Congress a proposal that would amend the Constitution to expand District voting in Congress. The proposal – H.J.Res. 396, introduced in the House by Representative Emanuel Celler – sought to authorize one voting Representative and granted Congress the authority to provide by legislation for additional representation in the House and Senate, up to that to which the District would be entitled were it a state.[31] The House Committee on the Judiciary held hearings on the Johnson proposal, as well as others, in July and August 1967.[32] The committee reported out an amended version of the resolution on October 24, 1967, which all owed full representation for the District of Columbia: two Senators and the number of Representatives to which it would be entitled if it were a state (two with its 1967 population of 763,000).[33] No other action was taken on the resolution during the 90th Congress.

Representative Don Edwards introduced the proposed constitutional amendment as H.J.Res. 554 in the 95th Congress on July 25, 1977.[34] It passed the House on March 2, 1978, by a 289-127 margin. On August 22, 1978, the Senate approved the resolution by a 57-32. The proposed amendment, having been passed by at least two-thirds of each house, was sent to the states. The amendment provided that – for the purposes of electing members of the U.S. Senate and House of Representatives and presidential electors, and for ratifying amendments to the U.S. Constitution – the District of Columbia would be considered as if it were a state. Under the Constitution, a proposed amendment requires ratification by three-fourths of the states to

---

at which point the size of the House of Representatives would be reset at 435. For additional analysis of the size of the House of Representatives, see CRS Report 95-791 GOV, *House of Representatives: Setting the Size at 435*, by David C. Huckabee.

[31] Congress was to resolve by appropriate legislation such questions as whether the House should be increased by the number of Representatives elected from the District, or whether it should temporarily increase and then revert to the statutory total of 435 after the 1970 census, as was done after Alaska and Hawaii achieved statehood in 1959 and 1960, respectively.

[32] "Major Legislation: D.C. Reorganization," *1967 CQ Almanac* (Washington: Congressional Quarterly Inc, 1968), p. 1026. According to the almanac: "The [1967 House and Senate Judiciary Committee] hearings marked the 19th time Congress had considered amendments giving Washington residents voting representation in Congress."

[33] U.S. Congress, Committee on the Judiciary, *Representation of the District o f Columbia*, report to accompany H.J.Res. 396, 90th Cong., 1st sess., H.Rept. 90-819 (Washington: GPO, 1967).

[34] 92 Stat. 3795. U.S. Congress, House Committee on the Judiciary, *District of Columbia Representation in* Congress, report to accompany H.J.Res. 554, 95th Cong., 2d sess., H.Rept. 95-886 (Washington: GPO, 1978). See also, "District of Columbia Representation in Congress," *Congressional Record*, vol. 124, March 2, 1978, pp. 5263-5273.

take effect. In addition, Congress required state legislatures to act on ratification in a seven-year period. The D.C. Voting Rights Amendment was ratified by 16 states, but expired in 1985 without winning the support of the requisite number of states (38).[35]

On June 3, 1992, Representative James Moran introduced H.J.Res. 501 (102nd Congress), a proposed constitutional amendment that declares that the District, which constitutes the seat of government of the United States, be treated as though it were a state for purposes of representation in Congress, election of the President and Vice President, and Article V of the Constitution. The resolution was referred to the House Judiciary Committee, where no action was taken. On July 14, 1998, Delegate Eleanor Holmes Norton introduced H.R. 4208 (105th Congress), a bill to provide for full voting representation in Congress for the District of Columbia. The bill was referred to the Committee on Judiciary, Subcommittee on the Constitution, where no action was taken.

Arguments for District Voting Representation in Congress Equivalent to That of States

Many of the arguments for District voting in Congress are similar to those in support of District statehood, i.e., the need for fairness to citizens in a representative democracy. Among the arguments for District voting are:

- District voting in Congress would elevate District residents to a level of participatory democracy on par with their counterpart American citizens in the 50 states. Currently, District residents are not allowed to participate in the national legislature as are their fellow Americans in the states because they are not represented in Congress in the same way as fellow citizens. District residents have no voice on issues such as the ratification of treaties and the confirmation of presidential appointees, particularly Cabinet secretaries and justices on the Supreme Court. In that regard, District voting in Congress would clarify the citizenship status of Americans who reside in the nation's capital.
- District voting in Congress would more fully symbolize the fundamental representative democracy that was envisioned by the

---

[35] The proposed D.C. voting rights amendment was ratified (in order) by: New Jersey, Michigan, Ohio, Minnesota, Massachusetts, Connecticut, Wisconsin, Maryland, Hawaii, Oregon, Maine, West Virginia, Rhode Island, Iowa, Louisiana, and Delaware.

framers of the Constitution. Representative democracies operate from the premise that they derive their authority from the consent of the governed. The American Revolution was fought so that basic political rights would be accorded to Colonial citizens, including no taxation without representation. District residents currently pay federal income tax, but have no voting representation in the legislative body that sets national tax policy.

- District voting in Congress would strengthen access to the democratic process for its residents. District residents carry the same burdens of citizenship as other Americans, such as federal taxation and fighting in wars, but have no vote in the national legislature that makes decisions that impact them.[36] The national legislators that make decisions regarding the District are not directly accountable to District residents.

Arguments against District Voting Representation in Congress Equivalent to That of States

Opponents of District voting representation in Congress base their position on constitutional grounds:

- The Constitution limits voting in Congress to representatives of the states. As the District is not a state, it is constitutionally prohibited from voting in Congress. Also in that regard, Article V of the Constitution prohibits representation for the District. The Article provides that "no State, without its Consent, shall be deprived of its equal suffrage in the Senate." The proviso was included to assure the smaller States that the larger States would not change the mode of representation in the Senate and thereby deprive them of their equal voice in that body. District voting in Congress would contravene this proviso.

- Opponents contend that because the Constitution is silent on the question of District voting in Congress, it was never intended that District residents would have voting representation in Congress.

---

[36] Given the District's symbolism as the nation's capital, it also carries the additional burden of being a prime target for terrorism.

- Granting voting representation in Congress would render the District over-represented in the national legislature, as all Members of Congress have constitutional oversight responsibility for the nation's capital. Further, a sizable number of District residents maintain a voting residence in another State; or, in the case of foreign diplomatic personnel accredited to Washington, in another country.

Option 2: Statehood

Statehood for the District of Columbia would settle the question of congressional representation for District residents. As a state, the District would have two Senators and at least one Representative, depending on population. Local efforts to have the District admitted as a State are long-standing, and legislation to do so has centered around making the non-federal land in the District of Columbia the nation's 51st state.

As the seven-year ratification period for the constitutional amendment proposed by H. J.Res. 554 drew near – with sufficient evidence that it would not succeed – the attention and efforts of local leaders shifted to an effort to make the District the 51st state. Many District critics of "home rule" and attempts to expand local representation through the 1978 Voting Rights Amendment contended that these attempts to expand local autonomy and increase congressional representation did not go far enough toward bringing the District full self-determination. Many in this group believed that statehood was the only way for the District to enjoy full congressional representation on a par with the states. Consequently, since 1983 there has been a continuing effort to bring statehood to the District – an effort that was most intense from 1987 through 1993. Since the 98th Congress, 13 statehood bills have been introduced.[37] On two occasions, House bills were reported out of the committee of jurisdiction, resulting in one floor vote.

---

[37] In the 98th Congress, Delegate Fauntroy introduced H.R. 3861 on Sept. 12, 1983, and Sen. Kennedy introduced S. 2672 on May 15, 1984. In the 99th Congress, Fauntroy introduced H.R. 325 on Jan. 3, 1985; Kennedy introduced S. 293 on Jan, 24, 1985. In the 100th Congress, Fauntroy introduced H.R. 51 on Jan. 6, 1987; Kennedy introduced S, 863 on March 26, 1987. In the 101st Congress, Fauntroy introduced H.R. 51 on Jan. 3, 1989; Kennedy introduced S. 2647 on May 17, 1990. In the 102nd Congress, Delegate Norton introduced H.R. 2482 on May 29, 1991; Kennedy introduced S. 2023 on Nov. 22, 1991. In the 103rd Congress, Norton introduced H.R. 51 on Jan. 5, 1993; Kennedy introduced S. 898 on May 5, 1993. In the 104th Congress, Norton introduced H.R. 51 on Jan. 4, 1995.

D.C. Delegate Walter E. Fauntroy introduced H.R. 51 in 1987 to create a state that would have encompassed only the non-federal land in the District of Columbia.[38] While the bill was reported out of the House District Committee, no vote was taken on the House floor. On a second statehood bill H.R. 51, introduced by Delegate Eleanor Holmes Norton in 1993, the measure was reported from the Committee on the District of Columbia,[39] and a vote was taken on the House floor on November 21, 1993, with a tally of 277-153 against passage.

Arguments for Statehood

Statehood supporters seek equity and equality vis-a-vis their fellow citizens around the country. They base their position on constitutional and economic grounds.

Constitutionally, they make three main arguments:

- Supporters argue that there is no constitutional bar preventing a state from existing within the District of Columbia. Further, as the Constitution grants Congress exclusive legislative authority over the District, it may be argued that Congress has the power to create any form of government it chooses.[40] That power could extend to the creation of a state government, as long as the federal enclave remains intact[41] because the language of the Constitution grants Congress exclusive authority over the district that became the seat of government, not just over the seat of government.[42]
- Supporters also note that the denial of full voting representation in Congress District residents conflicts with American principles of representative democracy. District residents carry the same burdens of citizenship as other Americans, such as federal taxation and

---

[38] Delegate Fauntroy introduced H.R. 51 on Jan. 6, 1987. U.S. Congress, Committee on the District of Columbia, *New Columbia Admission Act*, report to accompany H.R. 51, 100th Cong., 1st sess., H.Rept. 100-305 (Washington; GPO, 1987).

[39] U.S. Congress, Committee on the District of Columbia, *New Columbia Admission Act*, report to accompany H.R. 51, 103rd Cong., 1st sess., H.Rept. 103-371 (Washington: GPO, 1993).

[40] For a legal discussion of Congress and its potential power regarding District statehood, see: Peter Raven-Hansen, "The Constitutionality of D.C. Statehood," *The George Washington Law Review*, 60 Geo. Wash. L. Rev. 160 (1991).

[41] U.S. Congress, House Committee on the District of Columbia, *New Columbia Admission Act*, report to accompany H.R. 51, 100th Cong., 1st Sess., H.Rept. 100-305 (Washington: GPO, 1987), p. 21.

[42] Raven-Hansen, p. 166.

fighting in wars, yet they have no representation in the Senate and a non-voting Delegate in the House of Representatives. Supporters point out that no other democracy in the world denies voting representation in the national legislature to residents of its national capital.[43]

- Proponents of D.C. statehood also cite taxation without representation for District residents as a source of contention. Congress makes decisions that affect both the District and the states. District-specific decisions are made by Representatives who are not accountable to its residents. Conversely, decisions that affect the states are beyond the reach of the District.

In terms of economic viability, supporters have noted that the District compares favorably with many states. As shown in Table 1, earnings by industry within the District are diverse and rank higher than many states in several categories: in total gross state product – the gross market value of the goods and services attributable to labor and property located in a state – the District ranks higher than 14 states; in business starts, the District ranks higher than 11 states; and in general local governmental revenue, the District ranks higher than 17 states.

---

[43] U.S. Department of Justice, Office of Legal Policy, *Report to the Attorney General on the Question of Statehood for the District of Columbia* (Washington: April 3, 1987), pp. 42-43. See also, Charles W. Harris, *Congress and the Governance of the Nation's Capital: The Conflict of Federal and Local Interests* (Washington: Georgetown University Press, 1995), pp. 239-262.

Table 1. Selected D.C. Economic Indicators (in mlns of $)

Economic Attribute	District of Columbia	DC ranked higher than the following states in 1997
Total gross state product	$44,000.1	AK, DE, HI, ID, ME, MT, NH, NM, ND, RI, SD, VT, WV, WY
Business starts	696 starts	AK, DE, ME, MT, NE, ND, RI, SD, VT, WV, WY
General Local Government Revenue (1996)	$5,675.0	AK, AR, DE, HI, ID, ME, MT, NV, NH, NM, ND, RI, SD, UT, VT, WV, WY

Source: U.S. Census Bureau, *Statistical Abstract of the United States: 2000*, 120th Edition, (Washington: 2000). Total gross state product: table 720, p. 455; business starts: table 876, p. 548; and 1996 general local governmental revenue: table 514, p. 322.

Arguments against Statehood

Opponents of statehood argue that the District cannot be viable as a state – constitutionally and economically. They have cited concerns about the constitutional implications of such a move; the size, population, and economic viability of the proposed state; and the current level of congressional representation afforded the District.

Opponents make three main constitutional arguments:

- First, they argue that granting statehood would violate Article 1, Section 8, Clause 17, which designates a federal district to house the national capital. A neutral federal district was created to provide a jurisdiction in which Congress would have exclusive control.

- Second, some opponents argue that Article 4, section 3, clause 1, which provides that no new state shall be created within an existing state without the consent of the legislatures concerned, implies that the consent of Maryland would be necessary to create a state out of its former territory. They point to the terms under which Maryland ceded the land to create the federal district – that Maryland ceded land only to create a national seat of government.[44]

---

[44] 2 Laws of Maryland 1791, ch. 45, §2 (Kilty 1800). The Maryland law that ceded the territory stated, in part:
> That all that part of the said territory, called Columbia, which lies within the limits of this state, shall be and the same is hereby acknowledged to be forever ceded and relinquished to the congress and government of the United States, in

- Third, constitutional concern centers around the 23rd Amendment, which requires that the District of Columbia appoint three electors to the electoral college. Statehood for the District would require the amendment to be repealed or amended; otherwise, were the District to become a state, only a handful of citizens remaining in the federal enclave would control three electoral votes.

Economically, critics of D.C. statehood also contend that the small population and land mass render the District without the economic base to support statehood. Opponents have noted the fact that the District does not have a rural area as the other states do. Further concern has been raised about the District's economy being so closely tied to the presence of the Federal government. In this regard, critics of D.C. statehood contend that the District does not have a sufficiently diversified economy as can be found in other states.

On the question of current congressional representation, critics of D.C. statehood contend that the interests of the District are represented in several committees in both the House and Senate; therefore, no further congressional representation is needed.[45]

Option 3: Retrocession

Retrocession to Maryland of the non-federal land currently located in the District of Columbia would make District residents eligible to select congressional representatives as citizens of the state of Maryland. There is a precedent for retrocession of land. In 1846, District territory that lay west of the Potomac River (now the environs of Arlington County and the city of Alexandria) was retroceded to the state of Virginia. The impetus for the retrocession came from residents of the retroceded area. Largely because Virginia agreed to the retrocession, there was no constitutional challenge to the change. In the case of the current District of Columbia, however, some D.C. residents and some in the state of Maryland oppose retrocession.[46]

---

full and absolute right, and exclusive jurisdiction, as well of soil as of persons residing, or to reside, thereon, pursuant to the tenor and effect of the eighth section of the first article of the constitution of the government of the United States.

[45] *Report to the Attorney General on the Question of Statehood for the District of Columbia*, pp. 5-6.
[46] John E. Smith, "Statehood Alternatives Proposed," *The Washington Post*, March 6, 1990, B3.

Further, as the issue has not been judicially tested, Congress may not be able to compel Maryland to again assume jurisdiction over this territory.

Proponents of retrocession argue that returning the non-federal portion of the District of Columbia to Maryland and retaining a federal enclave for the seat of the national government would satisfy constitutional provisions regarding the seat of government.[47] Concomitantly, it would afford District residents voting representation in the U.S. House and Senate through the state of Maryland.

There may be a potential problem with retrocession as it affects perceptions of the national capital. Though many of the original reasons why a separate federal district was originally established are no longer applicable, "there is a widespread belief that the nation's capital should belong to the nation as a whole and should not be part of a particular state."[48] Consequently, retroceding the District to Maryland may be problematic for the rest of the country.

Since the 101st Congress, there have been seven bills introduced that would retrocede the District to the state of Maryland.[49] The bills would maintain exclusive legislative authority and control of Congress over the National Capital Service Area in the District of Columbia. No hearings or votes have been held on these bills.

Retrocession of the District to Maryland raises three important questions: Can Maryland be forced to take on the new territory if it opposes retrocession? What happens to the 23rd Amendment? What entity would provide public services (such as police and fire protection, trash removal, and road repair) to the federal enclave that would remain under congressional jurisdiction?

---

[47] The federal enclave currently has a small number of residents who, presumably, would control the three presidential electoral votes accorded the District by the 23rd Amendment. Consequently, any retrocession measure would have to address the utility of having a small number of citizens (fewer than 5,000) with a disproportionately large role in a presidential election.

[48] Lawrence M. Frankel, "National Representation for the District of Columbia: A Legislative Solution," 139 U. Pa. L. Rev. 1659 (1991): "for example, it is unlikely that the federal government needs a separate federal district in order to protect itself."

[49] In the 101st Congress, Rep. Regula introduced H.R. 4195 on March 6, 1990. In the 102nd Congress, Regula introduced H.R. 1204 on Feb. 28, 1991. In the 103rd Congress, Regula introduced H.R. 1205 on Mar. 3, 1993. In the 104th Congress, Regula introduced H.R. 1028 on Feb. 23, 1995. In the 105th Congress, Regula introduced H.R. 831 on Feb. 25, 1997. In the 106th Congress, Regula introduced H.R. 558 on Feb. 3, 1999. In the 107th Congress, Regula introduced H.R. 810 on Mar. 9, 2001.

As no state has been forced to accept a retrocession, the question is judicially and politically untested. Consequently, it is not known if the state of Maryland can be forced to take on its former territory.

The 23rd Amendment grants the District the right to appoint a "number of electors of President and Vice President equal to the whole number of Senators and Representatives in Congress to which the District would be entitled if it were a State ... they shall be in addition to those appointed by the States, but they shall be considered, for the purposes of the election of President and Vice President, to be electors appointed by a State...." Regarding the 23rd Amendment, one of two options could be taken: maintain the status quo, or abolish the amendment. Maintaining the status quo would give control of the three electoral votes allocated to the District of Columbia to the handful of citizens who would continue to live in the federal enclave.

The alternate to that situation would be to abolish the 23rd Amendment, which contains the proviso for three electoral votes.

The government of the District of Columbia provides the range of public services found in any other city. Retroceding the non-federal portion of the District to Maryland may leave the federal enclave without such services. While there are numerous federal police forces currently available that could be utilized to protect the federal enclave, an administrative entity of some sort might have to be created to oversee and manage other public services, such as firefighting, water and sewer service, road construction and rehabilitation. Some services could be contracted for, while others may not.

Option 4: District Residents Voting in Maryland

This option would allow District residents – for the purposes of representation in Congress and election of the President and Vice President – to be treated as citizens of, and vote in federal elections in, the state of Maryland in accordance with state law. It would also allow residents of the District of Columbia to have one Representative from the District in the House of Representatives and have their vote counted in the election of the two Senators from Maryland. Further, for purposes of determining eligibility to serve as a member of the House of Representatives or the Senate, a resident of the District of Columbia would have been considered an inhabitant of the state of Maryland.

One such bill was introduced to allow District residents to vote in federal elections as Maryland residents: H.R. 4193, introduced on March 6,

1990 by Representative Stanford Parris. The bill would have given the District a seat in the House of Representatives and given its residents the right to cast ballots in Maryland's Senate elections. It also would have maintained the District's governmental structure, and was offered "as a workable way to change the [status quo] which represents taxation without representation."[50]

District officials, along with some members of the House, opposed the bill, contending that it was not a practical solution to the District's representative concerns and that it would further cloud the District's status.

The proposal raises a number of questions of constitutional law, apportionment, and House procedure.[51] As the measure would have left the District intact as a congressional district, presumably regardless of its population, "one-person, one-vote" concerns could be raised.[52] The District's population is less than each of Maryland's congressional districts, giving District voters more voting representation than citizens in the state's other districts. Further, as the proposal does not make the District a state, it could be in violation of Article 1, Section 2 and the 14th Amendment. Article 1, Section 2 requires representatives to be chosen by the states. The 14th Amendment is the basis for the "one-person, one-vote" rulings on states' redistricting. In terms of House procedure, the proposal would have had to address the issue of size of the House and whether it would be expanded, temporarily or permanently, to accommodate a Representative from the District.

Congress took no action on the bill.

NO TAXATION WITHOUT REPRESENTATION ACT OF 2001 AND ISSUES FOR THE 107TH CONGRESS

Delegate Norton (H.R. 1193) and Senator Lieberman (S. 603) introduced the "No Taxation Without Representation Act of 2001" in March 2001. The bills would provide full voting representation in Congress for citizens of the District of Columbia, and would amend the Internal Revenue

---

[50] Kent Jenkins Jr., "Parris Bill Would Let D.C. Vote in Maryland Senate Race," *The Washington Post*, March 7, 1990, D1.
[51] Benjamin Sheffner, "Gingrich Plan to Give District Seat in Maryland Opens Pandora's Box: 436 Members? No Electoral Votes?" *Roll Call*, April 20, 1995, p. 1.
[52] Ibid.

Code of 1986 to exempt residents of the District from federal income taxation until such full voting representation takes effect.

While the proposed legislation does not define full representation, past efforts to increase congressional representation for the District have sought proportional representation in the House and two Senators.

Issues Raised by the Proposal

There appear to be two issues for Congress to consider in any action on the bill: the cost to the federal treasury for exempting District residents from federal individual income taxation; and the resolution of the constitutional questions regarding District voting.

Cost to Federal Treasury

Cost to the federal Treasury for exempting District residents from federal individual income taxation might be a factor were Congress to consider the bill. Table 2 shows the amount of revenue that would have been forgone had such an exemption from individual taxation been in place from 1995 through 1999. The table also shows the relative importance of the forgone tax revenues compared to all federal income tax receipts for each of the five years.

**Table 2. Federal Individual Income Taxes
Paid by District Residents, 1995-1999 (in mlns of $)**

	1995	1996	1997	1998	1999
Individual Federal Income Taxes Paid	1,737	1,843	2,058	2,235	2,515
Percentage of all Federal Income Tax Receipts	0.279%	0.265%	0.267%	0.269%	0.273%

Source: U.S. Internal Revenue Service, *Statistics of Income Bulletin*, 1996-2001.

Constitutional Questions

The Constitution requires that Members of Congress be elected by the people of the states, but the District is not a state. Given this language, Congress is limited in what it can do to increase voting representation in Congress for the District. It has been suggested that the most Congress may be able to do is create Delegate positions in the Senate to complement that of the House. As indicated above, there does not seem to be a constitutional bar to such a change. Otherwise, a constitutional amendment would be needed to give the District the full voting rights that it seeks in H.R. 1193.

Alternatives Short of Full Congressional Voting

In addition to this legislation, Congress could consider alternatives that would increase the District's current congressional representation, but fall short of proportional representation in the House and two Senators. In this regard, there are two variants of the voting representation in Congress option that could be offered as alternatives to the "No Taxation without Representation Act." The alternatives do not require constitutional amendment, but would enhance the District's representation in Congress. The first would grant the District's Delegate to the House a vote in the Committee of the Whole. This option is controversial because of the constitutional ramifications of having representatives of non-states voting in the Committee of the Whole.

At the start of the 103rd Congress, as with all new Congresses, a number of rule changes were adopted relating to the organization of the House. One such change affected Rule XII, and allowed Delegates and the Resident Commissioner of Puerto Rico to vote in the Committee of the Whole. The rule change was challenged in court on the grounds that the move was unconstitutional.[53] The claim of unconstitutionality rested on the argument that "these rules unconstitutionally vest the Delegates with legislative power, and that they dilute the legislative power of Members of the House."[54] Further, a claim was made that, in modifying the Delegates' role, the House violated the constitutional requirements of bicameralism and presentment of legislation to the President.[55] Ultimately, a U.S. district court upheld the provision allowing Delegate voting, but only because the rule provided that an immediate and automatic second ballot occur in cases where Delegate votes provided the margin of victory on a particular question. Under the rule, delegates were prohibited from participating in the second ballot. The district court decision was affirmed on appeal, and the question was rendered moot when the rule provision was rescinded at the start of the 104th Congress.

---

[53] *Michel v. Anderson*, 817 F. Supp. 126.
[54] 817 F. Supp. 126, at 2.
[55] Id at 2.

The second variant would be to create one or two District Delegate positions in the Senate, much like that in the House. As there appears to be no constitutional bar to such an office, Congress could consider such a proposal. The concept of a Delegate to the Senate from the District of Columbia was first considered when Rep. Lucus Miller introduced H.R. 10542 on February 14, 1893. The bill proposed authorizing the election of two Delegates to Congress from the District, one to the Senate and one to the House. No action was taken on the bill following its referral to the House Committee on the District of Columbia, A similar bill was introduced in 1931 (S. 10) that authorized the presidentially appointed District government to designate officers to represent the District government on the floor of the Senate and House. The bill was initially referred to the Senate District Committee, but it was discharged to the Committee on Rules, where no action was taken.

A 1970 report of the House District Committee accompanying H.R. 18619 – a bill to authorize two Delegates (one to the Senate, one to the House) for the District of Columbia – maintained that no constitutional proscription regarding a Delegate to the Senate existed and that the same arguments for allowing Delegates to the House could be applied.[56] The bill passed the House on August 10, 1970, by a vote of 338 yeas and 23 nays.[57] The Senate version of the bill was not acted upon beyond referral to the Committee on the District of Columbia. An amendment was introduced during floor consideration of the Home Rule Act of 1973 regarding a Senate Delegate for the District. The amendment was agreed to by voice vote, but was not included in the House-Senate conference on the legislation.[58]

---

[56] U.S. Congress, House Committee on the District of Columbia, *Establishing Nonvoting Delegates for the District of Columbia to the Senate and to the House of Representatives*, report to accompany H.R. 18619, 91st Gong., 2nd Sess., H.Rept. 1384 (Washington: GPO, 1970), p. 53.
[57] For the debate and vote, see: *Congressional Record*, v. 116, Aug. 10, 1970, pp. 28040-28054.
[58] *Congressional Record*, v. 119, October 10, 1973, p. H8843.

APPENDIX A: NUMBER OF BILLS INTRODUCED BY OPTION, SINCE 1978

	House	Senate
Voting Rights	4	1
Statehood	7	6
Retrocession	7	0
Voting in Maryland	1	0

Chapter 4

DISTRICT OF COLUMBIA: A BRIEF HISTORY OF CONGRESSIONAL ACTIONS AFFECTING THE BOARD OF EDUCATION

Eugene Boyd and Carol Glover

ABSTRACT

During the 20th century Congress enacted five public laws that delineates power and responsibility for public education in the District of Columbia and define the role of the District of Columbia school board. These laws established an appointed Board of Education (1906); required popular election of school board members (1968); established the school board as an independent agency (1973); and gave authority to grant charters for charter schools (1995). A separate law in 1995 created an oversight panel (Control Board) charged with improving financial and management operations of the District government, including public education. A consequence of the 1995 law that created the Control Board was a temporary "takeover" of the District of Columbia Public Schools. Under the law the Control Board assumed much of the school board's responsibilities. This chapter provides a historical overview of the impact of federal legislation on the District of Columbia Board of Education with particular attention to the operation of the elected school board since 1968.

INTRODUCTION

Power and responsibility for public education in the District of Columbia and the role of the school board has been delineated in five public laws passed by Congress during this century. The Organic Act of 1906 established a Board of Education appointed by District of Columbia Court of Appeals judges. The District of Columbia Elected Board of Education Act of 1968 established the city's first elected school board. Five years later in 1973, Congress passed the District of Columbia Self-Government and Government Reorganization Act of 1973, which established the school board as an independent agency under the city's home rule charter. The Act also conveyed to the city's newly created and popularly elected city council the power to establish annual salaries for school board members. The School Reform Act of 1995 included provisions creating charter schools in the District of Columbia, and gave chartering authority to the Board of Education and an independent agency. Also in 1995, Congress passed the District of Columbia Financial Responsibility and Management Assistance Act of 1995, which created an oversight panel (Control Board) charged with improving financial and management operations of the District government, including public education.

In 1996, citing problems with the quality of public education, the Control Board stripped the elected school board of much of its authority and transferred it to an appointed advisory committee. The action of the Control Board was successfully challenged by the school board in court. In October of 1998, the school board and Control Board signed a memorandum of understanding that called for the return of the authority for public education to the school board by June 30, 2000.

In September 1999, the Appleseed Center, a nonprofit public interest organization, released a report entitled *Reforming the D.C. Board of Education: A Building Block for Better Public Schools*. The report called for a restructuring of the District of the Columbia Board of Education (DCBE). Although the report did not recommend a specific reform proposal it outlined several options.

Like other troubled urban school systems, during its 31 year history, the elected school board has been characterized by some observers as a body shaped by politics, the parochial interests of individual school board members, an often adversarial relationship with school superintendents, and an inability to ensure quality education for all District school children.

During this time, the District of Columbia Public Schools have experienced declining test scores, high dropout rates, parental dissatisfaction, congressional scrutiny, the creation of charter schools, and a Control Board takeover of the District's public schools.

SIGNIFICANT CONGRESSIONAL ACTIONS AFFECTING THE DISTRICT OF COLUMBIA BOARD OF EDUCATION

The Appointed School Board

The Organic Act of 1906, P.L. 55-254, signed by President Theodore Roosevelt on June 20, 1906, authorized the creation of a nine-member board of education for the District of Columbia public schools. The Act, as passed by the 55th Congress, gave the judges of the United States District Court for the District of Columbia the power to appoint members of the school board. Previously, school board members were appointed by the Commissioners of the District of Columbia. In accordance with the act, at least three of the appointed school board members were to be women. In addition, by custom, the board comprised six whites and three blacks. Board members must have been residents of the District for 5 years before appointment, served for 3 years, and received no financial compensation. The Board was responsible for the appointment of key education personnel, including the superintendent of public schools and his two assistants, an assistant superintendent for white schools, and an assistant superintendent for "Negro" schools.

The appointment of school board members by District Court judges was subsequently criticized. Critics contended that District judges, who themselves were appointed, were neither accountable to the community, nor responsible for the operation of the District government including its schools and other public services. A 1967 report by the Teachers College of Columbia University on the District schools, entitled *Toward Creating a Model Urban School System: A Study of the Washington, D.C. Public Schools,* detailed the criticisms of the method used to appoint school board members and the Court's view of its appointment duty. According to the report:

> ... the task of selecting Board members has been viewed as an unnecessary nuisance to be relegated to the most junior member of the court. That judge has usually had neither the time nor the inclination to evaluate carefully the

qualifications of incumbent Board members for reappointment nor the even more difficult and time-consuming job of screening new nominees. Consequently, the Court, until recently, tended to reappoint incumbents automatically rather than invest the energy necessary to produce a first-class Board.[59]

Hobson v. Hansen Court Challenge

By 1966, the District of Columbia public school population was approximately 90% black. In 1966, Julius Hobson, a noted civil rights activist and crusader for home rule for the District, filed suit against the superintendent of D.C. public schools, the appointed school board, and the District Court judges who appointed the school board. Hobson's suit charged that the District's schools deprived poor and black children of educational opportunities provided to white and more affluent students. Hobson's contention was that poor and black children received inferior educational services due to school system policies and practices relating to neighborhood based schools, faculty assignments, the use of tracking in the placement of students based on ability, optional school zones which allowed some students a choice of schools, overcrowded neighborhood schools, and inadequate funding for education.

In 1967, the District of Columbia Court of Appeals ruled in favor of Hobson, and directed the school board to undertake certain reforms, including abolishing the tracking system, abolishing optional school zones, providing transportation to school children in an effort to relieve overcrowding in neighborhood schools, and developing a plan for full integration of the school system teachers. Though the board acquiesced, the Superintendent of Public Schools, Carl F. Hansen, resigned in order to appeal the decision. In January 1969, the United States Court of Appeals for the District of Columbia upheld the lower court's decision.

District of Columbia Elected Board of Education Act of 1968, P.L. 90-292

District resident dissatisfaction with the public school governing structure, the court's disinterest in appointing school board members, the

---

[59] Passow, A. Harry. *Toward Creating A Model Urban School System: A Study of the Washington, D.C. Public Schools*. Teaches College Columbia University, 1967. p. 171.

absence of democratic selection of school board members, the decline in school performance, and the *Hobson v. Hansen* court challenge prompted Congress to enact legislation establishing an elected school board. In 1968, Congress passed P.L. 90-292, the District of Columbia Elected Board of Education Act of 1968. The Act provided for the election of an 11 member school board. Eight members of the board were elected on a geographical basis, one from each ward, and three elected at-large. The legislation called for staggered terms of 1, 3, and 4 years for the board members initially elected in 1968, and beginning with the 1973 elections all members of the board would serve 4-year terms. The elections were nonpartisan, however political parties were allowed to endorse candidates. This was the first election of local public officials in more than 100 years. The election of school board members was viewed by many as an initial step in the city's quest for home rule, which had been an active issue since the 1950s, but was opposed by the House District of Columbia Committee.

During the first election on November 5, 1968, 53 candidates ran for the eight ward seats and nine for the three at-large seats. Only one candidate, Julius Hobson, running at-large, amassed the required majority to win a seat on the board. On November 26, 1968, run-off elections were held to determine the final winners of the board's remaining eight ward and two at-large seats. The first school board election of 1968 initially generated great interest among the city's voters. Seventy percent of the registered voters cast ballots on November 5, 1968. However, during the runoff election only 26% of registered voters cast ballots. The creation of the school board was seen by many as a trial balloon testing the city's readiness for full home rule.

The 1968 Act delineated the powers and responsibilities of the elected school board to include: establishing general policies governing public schools; appointment of the school superintendent and other administrative officers; preparation of the school system's annual budget; election of the board's president and vice president; and the development of a committee structure to facilitate the board's carrying out its duties and responsibilities. The board, as constituted by the 1968 Act, the Organic Act of 1906, and the District of Columbia Self-Government and Governmental Reorganization Act (Home Rule Act) of 1973, also undertakes several functions traditionally performed by state education agencies (SEAs), including monitoring and administering all federal education grants, teacher certification, and special education programs and services. The District is the only city in the U.S. that has this added responsibility.

Home Rule Act of 1973, P.L. 93-198: Its Impact on the School Board

In 1973, Congress passed the Home Rule Act of 1973, P.L. 93-198. The Act established limited home rule for the District of Columbia. It provided for the popular election of a mayor, the District's chief executive officer; and a 13-member Council of the District of Columbia, the city council, the city's legislature. Section 495 of the Home Rule Act also maintained the Board of Education as an independent agency whose rules and policies cannot be overturned by the mayor or the city council. Although the school board is considered an independent entity, it lacks the authority to generate income through the use of taxing or bond authority. The mayor and the city council determine the aggregate amount of funds budgeted for public education, with the school board determining how such funds were spent. In addition, the city council does exercise some limited influence over public school policies through its Committee on Education. The mayor and the council may review, but cannot amend, the school board's budget. This organizational structure is common to many cities in the U.S. In 1995, as discussed further below, Congress created a Control Board and gave it wide-ranging powers and authority, including the power to veto, revise, or amend the District's budgetary priorities. Like all other aspects of the District's budget, Congress retains the power to veto, amend, or revise the District's budget, including its education funding.

Prior to the 1973 Home Rule Act, which allows citizens of the District of Columbia to elect the city's mayor and city council, the school board was the only elected local office chosen by democratic vote of the citizens of the city. Since the advent of home rule, the school board has served as a stepping stone for those aspiring to higher office. It has attracted the attention of politically active members of the city, a number of them later would run for mayor or the city council, including former Mayor Marion Barry and City Council Chair Linda Cropp, and former council members Hilda Mason, Frank Smith, and Betty Ann Kane, and council member Carol Schwartz.

The District of Columbia Financial Responsibility and Management Assistance Act of 1995, P.L. 104-8

In 1995, after years of financial mismanagement and poor service delivery, Congress stripped the city's local elected officials of much of their authority and power. In passing the District of Columbia Financial Responsibility and Management Assistance Act of 1995, P.L. 104-8, the Congress created a five-member District of Columbia Financial Responsibility and Management Assistance Authority (Control Board), charged with restoring the District to financial solvency and improving the delivery of services, including public education.

In November 1996, the Control Board fired Superintendent of Public Schools Franklin Smith and replaced him with retired General Julius Becton as CEO-Superintendent of the District of Columbia Public Schools (DCPS). In addition, the Control Board transferred control of the school system from the elected school board to an emergency board of trustees. The school board later successfully challenged the Control Board's authority to appoint an education oversight committee, arguing that the oversight committee lacked the authority of the Control Board to usurp the school board's powers. The Control Board's action followed years of parental dissatisfaction with the operation of public schools, as demonstrated by declining test scores, deteriorating facilities, and the failure to open schools on time.[60] The delayed school openings stemmed in large part from school officials' inability to satisfy a court order stemming from a suit by Parents United, requiring DCPS to address fire code hazards and other facilities maintenance issues.[61] At one time, the DCPS estimated that it would cost up to $90 million to fix fire code violations. Ironically, in 1998, CEO-Superintendent Becton's early resignation was in part precipitated by questions involving cost overruns in school roof repair projects.

---

[60] During a 4-year period from 1994 to 1998, the opening day of school was delayed each year because of repairs to school buildings.
[61] Parents United is a non-profit parent-based watchdog group advocating for reform in the District's public schools.

District of Columbia School Reform Act of 1995, P.L. 104-134

Passed as part of the Omnibus Balanced Budget Act of 1996, P.L. 104-134, the District of Columbia School Reform Act, included several provisions affecting public education in the District of Columbia. The Act gives the Control Board authority to act on issues affecting public education, directs the school board and superintendent of DCPS to develop a public education reform plan, requires the DCPS to submit to the General Accounting Office an annual report on enrollment by school, program, grade designation, and amount of nonresident tuition due and collected.

In addition, the Act authorized the creation of public charter schools in the District of Columbia, set forth requirements for certification as a public charter school, and identified the process for approving or denying public charter school petitions. Under the provisions of the Act, public charter schools could be established as new schools, or from existing public or private schools. Charters may be granted by the board of education, a public charter school board, or other entity that may be authorized by the city council. The D.C. School Reform Act allows each chartering authority to grant up to five charters per year, which the 1998 District of Columbia Appropriations Act increased to 10 per chartering authority per year. Since the passage of the School Reform Act, an independent charter school board and the elected school board have granted public charter school status to 28 schools. In 1998, approximately 3,600 students, 5% of the total student population in the District of Columbia, attended public charter schools.

District of Columbia charter schools are operated as independent local educational agencies (LEAs); they are granted complete control over school expenditures, and are exempt from many of the policies, rules, and regulations issued by the Superintendent of DCPS. They must meet requirements similar to those prescribed for the federal Public Charter Schools program (e.g., non-sectarian, comply with civil rights statutes, and admit students by lottery if oversubscribed). Charters can be revoked if terms of the charter are violated, or there is fiscal mismanagement. Only one of the 28 charters granted in the District has been revoked.

District of Columbia Appropriations Act for FY1998, P.L. 105-100 (Charter Schools)

Concerned about the failure of the District's schools to open on time in September 1997, for a fourth consecutive year, the District of Columbia Appropriations Act for FY1998 required the Control Board and the Superintendent to report to the relevant committees of Congress by April 1, 1998 on all actions necessary to ensure that the District's public schools open on time for the 1998-1999 academic year.

The District's FY1998 appropriations act contained a number of substantive provisions affecting public charter schools in the District. The annual number of charters that can be granted per chartering authority was increased from five to 10 schools. An annual deadline by which Chartering authorities must make a decision on new charter applications was established. The Board of Trustees was directed to report to the Congress, within 120 days of enactment, the capital needs of each charter school, and provide to charter schools financial assistance to meet capital needs equivalent to that provided to DCPS, including giving priority to charter schools in the disposition of surplus public school property. Any funds reserved for charter schools not expended by May 1, 1998, plus certain other funds that may become available, will be placed in a New Charter School Fund, a revolving loan fund to help charter schools meet startup costs.

District of Columbia Appropriations Act for FY1999, P.L. 105-277 (Special Education)

In August 1998, during testimony before the House Oversight Subcommittee on the District of Columbia, Constance Newman, a member of the Control Board, identified problems in the school system's special education program. The District public school system provides special education services to nearly 7,700 students, approximately 10% of the District's public school population. Following a nationwide trend, the number of students seeking special education assistance is expected to grow to 11,000 in the next several years. This growth in special education needs has implications for the future cost of education and the pace of educational reform. The school system has budgeted $167 million for special education services for FY1999, which is 30% of the school system's total budget.

In addition, delays in the period between the time a student is referred and assessed increase the number of students placed in private educational institutions, which adds to cost of special education. Concern about the cost of these delays prompted Congress to include a provision in the District of Columbia Appropriations Act for FY1999 that extends the time period between referral and assessment of a student with special education needs from 50 days to 120 days, and provided $30 million in funding to address the problems the backlog in referral and evaluations of students with special education needs.

On April 13, 1999, the District of Columbia City Council passed PR 13-113. The resolution establishes a special committee (Council Special Education Program Investigation Special Committee) to investigate the delivery of special education services, and includes all members of the City Council of District of Columbia. The resolution gives the Special Committee one year to investigate and recommend improvements in the delivery of services. In April 1999, the superintendent placed three of the agency's top special education administrators on administrative leave. The superintendent also announced administrative and program changes as part of a 90-day action plan intended to address some of the agency's longstanding problems, including transferring the responsibility for special education assessments to school principals.

REGAINING CONTROL: THE SCHOOL BOARD'S COURT CHALLENGE AND THE MEMORANDUM OF UNDERSTANDING

On January 6, 1998, the United States Court of Appeals for the District of Columbia Circuit overturned portions of a decision of the United States District Court for the District of Columbia in *Shook, et al. v. District of Columbia Financial Responsibility and Management Assistance Authority*. In filing suit against the Control Board over its takeover the public school system, the school board argued that the Control Board lacked the authority to transfer administrative responsibility to an emergency board of trustees. The Control Board countered that Section 207(d) of the District of Columbia School Reform Act of 1996, which amends the District of Columbia Financial Responsibility and Management Assistance Act of 1995, conveys to it the power to issue orders, rules, or regulations that are legally binding to the same extent as if issued by the mayor or the head of any department or agency of the District of Columbia, including the school board. The Appeals Court ruled that the Control Board may exercise direct control over the school system, but could not transfer to an advisory body, such as the emergency board of trustees, administrative control over the school system. The Appeals Court also found that the Control Board lacked the authority to dismiss then-Superintendent Franklin Smith at will.

In October 1998, the Control Board and the elected school board signed a memorandum of understanding that calls for the development of a transition plan that would allow the school board to regain control of the public schools. The memorandum also states that the Control Board and the Board of Education, with the advice of the trustees, superintendent, parents, and other citizens, must develop the plan for transferring power to the school board prior to the June 30, 2000 deadline. Under the memorandum, the Control Board designates the Board of Education, rather than the Board of Trustees, as the principal advisor to the Control Board for facilities planning and student discipline. The Emergency Board of Trustees remains the principal advisor for all other matters, including finance and academics. The transition period was deemed necessary by the Control Board to insure that the Board of Education is familiar with major changes in policy and practices instituted since November 1996, and is prepared to run the DCPS by June 2000.

In December 1998, the Authority created the D.C. Public School Board Transition Planning Team, to be lead by Mary Futrell, Ed.D., former president of the National Education Association, and former dean of the George Washington University Graduate School of Education and Human Development. Also on the six-member team are the president of the School Board, two lawyers, two parents of DCPS students, and two consultants specializing in transitions in education and management. The team issued its report in February 1999. The transition team developed its report based on the premise that the Board of Education's fundamental mission is to set policy, and that the Superintendent is responsible for its effective administration.

THE ELECTION OF 1998

On November 5, 1998, District voters also elected five members to the city's elected school board. They include Gail Dixon (At-large), Westy Byrd

(Ward 2), Tom Kelly (Ward 7), William Lockridge (Ward 8), and Dwight Singleton (Ward 4). None had served previously on the elected school board. The expectations for the five newly elected school board members were high.

Earlier this year, the block of newly elected school board members clashed with the board's chair, Wilma Harvey, over allegations that Harvey improperly used school board personnel for personal projects. The board, by a vote of 6 to 5, removed Wilma Harvey as chair of the Board of Education and replaced her with Dwight Singleton. However, Harvey challenged her removal. The District of Columbia Office of Corporation Counsel ruled that the Board of Education likely violated its own by-laws in removing Harvey. The Corporation Counsel noted that the board should have issued charges against Harvey before taking action. Subsequently, Harvey was replaced by Robert Childs, an at-large member of the Board.

Some observers of the Board of Education argue that the latest squabbling reflects poorly on the Board at a time when it should be focusing on school reform and the return of its policy making powers. This latest controversy has been compared to past school boards which some considered to be politicized and ineffective in attending to the education of the District's children. The chairmanship controversy jeopardized the scheduled June 30, 2000, transfer of administrative authority to the existing school board and refocused city and congressional attention on the need for reform.

REFORMING AND RESTRUCTURING THE SCHOOL BOARD

The mayor, city council, control board, and various constituencies in support of public schools agree on the need to reform the city's public school governing body – the Board of Education. The direction of school board reform in the District of Columbia, including the size of the school board and whether to elect or appoint school board members, has been hotly debated. A *Washington Post* poll earlier this year indicated that 54% of those polled favored an elected school board.

Appleseed Center Report on Reforming the Board of Education

Many of the issues surrounding elected-versus-appointed school boards were outlined in a September 9, 1999, report by the Appleseed Center[62] entitled *Reforming the D. C. Board of Education: A Building Block for Better Public Schools*. Much of the debate on elected-versus-appointed boards involves matters of accountability, democracy, efficacy, and expertise. Supporters of an elected board believe that such boards are directly accountable, and thus sensitive, to the concerns of the electorate because they are democratically elected. Detractors argue that elected boards, particularly those elected by ward or district, are too parochial in their focus, and too partisan in their politics. School boards, they contend, often serve as a political training ground for persons with higher political aspirations who are interested in building a political base. They argue that, historically, the District of Columbia Board of Education has served as a stepping stone to higher political office.

Supporters of appointed boards contend that appointed board members are more likely to bring education or other expertise to the board's deliberations, and are less likely to be swayed by partisan or parochial pressures to protect the interest of a particular group in order to win political advantage. Detractors argue that appointed boards are subject to patronage, and are selected in an undemocratic fashion.

The Appleseed Center's research supports three fundamental principles upon which to base reforms. They include:

- reducing the size of the Board of Education from its current 11 members to nine or fewer with all members elected, or all appointed, or some combination of the two (a so called hybrid board);

- in instances where board members are elected, requiring that any ward-based members (or those representing larger segments of the city) be elected in two steps: a primary conducted in each ward (or larger segment), followed by a citywide runoff among the top two vote-getters from each ward (or larger segment); and

---

[62] The Appleseed Center is nonprofit, nonpartisan, public interest organization dedicated to addressing systemic management and financial problems of the District of Columbia.

- in instances where members are appointed, requiring that the mayor appoint them from a list of nominees provided by a broad-based commission, and that those appointments be subject to D.C. Council approval.[63]

REFERENDUM ON SCHOOL BOARD GOVERNANCE

On February 17, 2000, after weeks of wrangling and several false starts, the city council, with the mayor's support, approved a bill (D.C. Act 13-295) that would restructure the District of Columbia Board of Education, pending approval of a referendum by District voters. The act, which amends the District's Home Rule Act, would:

- reduce the school board from the 11 to nine members;

- allow voters to elect four members of the board from four new school election districts (currently eight members of the board are elected by ward);

- allow voters to elect one at-large member to serve as President of the Board of Education; and

- allow the mayor to appoint four members to the board with the advice and consent of the city council.

The proposed hybrid board composed of elected and appointed members is a compromise proposal that, according public statements, has only lukewarm support of the mayor and many members of the city council. The mayor first rejected a proposal for a hybrid of February 1, 2000. The mayor's original proposal, which would have allowed him to appoint the superintendent and a five-member Board of Education, was soundly defeated by the council by a vote of 10 to two on January 18, 2000.

On February 17, 2000, the mayor and the council settled on the hybrid board compromise, after considering and rejecting proposals that:

---

[63] The complete Appleseed report may be viewed and downloaded from the internet at:

- transferred control of the schools, including the hiring and firing of the superintendent, to the mayor for a specific period after declaring a state of emergency, and then returning power to a restructured and smaller seven-member elected board;

- reduced the Board of Education from 11 to seven elected members; and

- allowed District residents to choose between a nine-member elected school board and a five-member board appointed by the mayor.

The latter proposal, which was initially approved by the city council on February 1, 2000, was roundly criticized by Alice Rivlin, Chair of the Control Board, who argued that a referendum fight over an elected-versus-appointed board would be divisive. She urged the council and the mayor to support a single plan or face the possibility of Control Board or congressional interference. Subsequently, the District of Columbia Board of Elections and Ethics informed the council in a letter dated February 14, 2000, that the act (PR 13-469) was "improper for submission to the electorate in its current form as a valid charter amendment." It suggested that the bill as structured improperly delegated a legislative function to the electorate. The proper function of the electorate, in this case, is to ratify or reject, by referendum, the actions of the city council. The Board of Elections and Ethics (BEE) noted that the charter amendment process,[64] unlike a voter-sponsored referendum,[65] does not provide for conflicting or multiple-choice measures to be considered by voters. Instead, the BEE suggested that the city council consider passing a *resolution*, not an act, calling for a special election to conduct an advisory referendum. The BEE noted several "advantages" of passing a resolution to call a special election, stating that resolutions, unlike acts, do not require control board review, and that the council can specify the date the referendum may be conducted.

[http://www.appleseeds.net/dc/governance.html].
[64] See DC Code §1-205. Charter amending procedure.
[65] See DC Code §1-1320(s). Initiative and referendum process.

Referendum Process and the Role of Congress

Due to budget constraints, low turnout concerns, and a busy election schedule, the BEE would prefer conducting the referendum during the November general election. A special election has been set for June 27, 2000, for voters to consider the referendum. The BEE regulations require that a minimum of 54 days must expire after the BEE certifies the referendum question. It held a public meeting on Tuesday, May 2, 2000, to hear public comment and formulate the final short title and summary statement for the Proposed Charter Amendment III, "The School Governance Charter Amendment Act of 2000." Upon completion of this exercise the BEE certified the referendum question, which will ask D.C. voters for a yes or no vote in support of creation of a hybrid school board. The BEE has estimated the costs of conducting the special election at approximately $371,000. Should the voters approve the ballot question on June 27, 2000, candidates for the five elected seats on the new school board could pick up their petitions on July 7, 2000. The petitions must be returned by August 30, 2000, in order for a candidate to appear on the November 7, 2000 general election ballot. If the charter amendment is rejected by the voters, the school board would continue as presently structured, an 11 member elected board, with six board members facing reelection in the November 7, 2000 general election.

DC Code §1-205 outlines the process to be used to modify or amend the District of Columbia Self-Government and Governmental Reorganization Act of 1973, P.L. 9-198 (Home Rule Act). The present proposal (D.C. Act 13-295), which was approved by the council on February 17, 2000, would change the number and method of selecting members of the Board of Education as described in Title IV, Part F, Sec. 495 of the Home Rule Act. The following is a summary of the referendum process as outlined in DC Code § 1-205.

Step one: The city council approves the measure.

Step two: The measure must be ratified by simple majority of the voters.

Step three: If the measure is approved by the voters, BEE must certify that the charter amendment has been ratified by the voters and forward the charter amendment to the Speaker of the

Step four: House and the President of the Senate on the same day of the BEE certification.

Congress gets 35 calendar days (excluding Saturdays, Sundays, holidays, and days on which either house of Congress is not in session) to review the proposal. If Congress supports the proposal, no action needs to be taken. If Congress opposes the action then it must pass a joint resolution of disapproval. If both houses of Congress consider and pass a joint resolution of disapproval, the proposed charter amendment is considered repealed upon expiration of the 35 day period.

DC Code §1-207 further prescribes the procedures and time line for House and Senate consideration of a joint resolution of disapproval. Essentially, DC Code §1-207 sets forth two possible courses of congressional action with respect to the disposition of the joint resolution of disapproval. The measure may be reported out of the House and Senate committees of jurisdiction, or it may be the subject of a motion to discharge the committee from further consideration (See Table 1).

Alternative Congressional Action

Alternatively, Congress may enact school board reforms through direct action. It has the power under Sec. 8 of Article 1 of the United States Constitution as outlined under Title IV, Reservation of Congressional Authority, of the Home Rule Act and under DC Code §1-206, which states:

Table 1: Disposition of a Joint Resolution of Disapproval

Scenario A: If Reported out of Committee		Scenario B: If Discharged from Committee	
Action	**Time frame**	**Action**	**Time frame**
Joint resolution disapproving the charter amendment is *introduced*.	At any time after receipt of the certification of the vote by the BEE, and within 35 day thereafter.*	Joint resolution disapproving the charter amendment is *introduced*.	At anytime after receipt of the certification of the vote by the BEE, and within 35 day thereafter.*
Joint resolution is referred to House and Senate authorizing committees on the District of Columbia.	Same day joint resolution is introduced.	Measure referred to House and Senate committees on the District of Columbia.	Joint resolution disapproving the charter amendment is *introduced*.
Committee *reports* the joint resolution disapproving the charter amendment.	Joint resolution may be reported at any time after being referred to committee but no later than the 35th day after receipt of the certification from the BEE.	Motion to discharge a committee from further consideration of the joint resolution of disapproval can be offered only by a supporter of the joint resolution of disapproval. If the motion is agreed to, committee is discharged from further consideration of the joint resolution of disapproval.†	Discharge motion cannot be offered until more than 20 calendar days have passed since the joint resolution was introduced, nor if the joint resolution has been reported or more than 35 days have elapsed since receipt of the charter amendment. Motion can be debated for up to one hour.
Motion to *consider* the joint resolution can be offered.‡	Motion is not debatable.	If discharge motion is adopted, motion to consider the joint resolution can be offered. Vote on motion to discharge.‡	Motion is not debatable.

Scenario A: If Reported out of Committee		Scenario B: If Discharged from Committee	
Action	Time frame	Action	Time frame
If motion to consider is adopted, joint resolution is considered and voted on.§	Debate on the joint resolution cannot exceed 10 hours. Vote on joint resolution must occur within 35 days of the introduction of the charter amendment.	If motion to consider is adopted, joint resolution is considered and voted on.§	Debate on the joint resolution cannot exceed 10 hours. Vote on joint resolution must occur within 35 days of the introduction of the charter amendment.

Note: Actions described would occur in each House separately.

* 35 day period excludes Saturdays, Sundays, holidays, and days when either house of Congress is not in session.

† Discharge motion cannot be amended or reconsidered. If voted on, no other discharge motion on a joint resolution addressing the same charter amendment may be considered.

‡ The motion may not be amended or reconsidered If rejected, it may be repeated.

§ Joint resolution may not be amended or recommitted. Vote on joint resolution may not be reconsidered.

§1-206. Congressional reservation of authority
Notwithstanding any other provision of this Act, the Congress of the United States reserves the right, at any time, to exercise its constitutional authority as legislature for the District, by enacting legislation for the District on any subject, whether within or without the scope of legislative power granted to the Council by the Act, including legislation to amend or repeal any law in force in the District prior to or after enactment of this Act and any act passed by the Council.

SCHOOL BOARD COMPENSATION

The issue of compensation for school board members has been hotly debated. In the early 1980s, the compensation paid to school board members far exceeded that paid by other jurisdictions with student populations of similar size, according to a June 6, 1982 publication of the District of Columbia League of Women Voters.[66] In 1982, members of the District's school board received annual compensation of $19,656 with the president of the board receiving $22,152. By 1996, board members received an annual salary of $30,000 and the president receiving salary compensation of $32,000.

Prior to 1995, the year Congress created the District of Columbia Financial Responsibility and Management Assistance Authority (the Control Board), the power to set salaries for board members resided with the District of Columbia City Council under Chapter 31-101(b)(2) of the DC Code. In 1996, the Control Board stripped the school board of much of its policy and administrative authority and reduced annual salaries of board members by 50%. Under Chapter 1-612.10 of the DC Code, members of the District of Columbia School Board may receive an annual salary of not more than $15,000, and the president of the board may receive an annual salary of $16,000. These sums may not be increased without the approval of the city council.

---

[66] *League of Women Voters of the District of Columbia, Study and Action,* The D.C. Board of Education. June 1982. p. 4.

Chapter 5

DISTRICT OF COLUMBIA TUITION ASSISTANCE PROGRAM

Bonnie Mangan

ABSTRACT

The District of Columbia College Access Act of 1999 (H.R. 974), enacted on November 12, 1999 (P.L. 106-98), created the District of Columbia (D.C.) Tuition Assistance Program. The D.C. Tuition Assistance Program provides scholarships for undergraduate education to District of Columbia residents ranging from $2,500 to $10,000. Scholarships may be used to attend public higher education institutions throughout the country, as well as some private institutions. Originally, the program was limited to providing scholarships for attending public higher education institutions in Maryland and Virginia, but it was expanded to include public institutions nationwide in May 2000. The program awarded grants to approximately 3,200 applicants during 2000. On March 14, 2002, Congress passed the District of Columbia College Access Improvement Act of 2002 (P.L. 107-157), to allow more D.C. residents to participate in the program.

SCHOLARSHIP AWARDS

The District of Columbia College Access Act of 1999 (H.R. 974), enacted on November 12, 1999 (P.L. 106-98), created the District of Columbia (D.C.) Tuition Assistance Program, which provides scholarships to D.C. residents for their undergraduate education. Initially, these scholarships could be used to pay the cost of attendance at public institutions of higher education in Maryland and Virginia. In May 2000, the program was expanded to include such institutions nationwide. Scholarships for public higher education institutions in all 50 states are used to pay the difference between in-state and out-of-state tuition, up to $10,000 per student per school year (with a cumulative cap of $50,000 per student). Initially, scholarships of $2,500 per student per year (with a cumulative cap of $12,500 per student) were available for tuition at a limited number of private Historically Black Colleges and Universities (HBCUs) in Maryland and Virginia, Under P.L. 107-157, students attending private HBCUs nationwide may now receive the tuition grants.

In the event that the amount of funds needed to cover approved applications exceeds the annual appropriation, scholarships will be reduced based on each applicant's financial need, with returning applicants receiving preference over new applicants.

ELIGIBILITY FOR SCHOLARSHIPS

The District of Columbia College Access Improvement Act (P.L. 107-157) revises the eligibility requirements and expands the benefit for District students. This legislation amends the current Act to permit individuals who graduated from secondary schools prior to 1998 and individuals who enroll in an institution of higher education more than 3 years after graduating from a secondary school to participate in the Tuition Assistance Program.

Students who graduated from secondary school or received the equivalent of a high school diploma before January 1, 1998 and are currently enrolled at an eligible institution may participate in the tuition assistance program.[67] They must meet the residency requirement of having lived in the District of Columbia for 12 consecutive months prior to the start of their freshman year at college. For individuals who graduated from secondary school prior to 1998 and never attended college or individuals re-enrolling after more than a 3-year break in post secondary education, the D.C. residency requirement is 5 consecutive years.[68]

---

[67] P.L. 107-157 §2 (A) (ii).
[68] P.L. 107-157 §2 (A) (iii).

P.L. 107-157 closes a loophole that allowed non-U.S. citizens residing in the District of Columbia to receive the tuition assistance benefit. Under the revised legislation, students applying for tuition assistance must meet citizenship and immigration status requirements under Section 484(a)(5) of the Higher Education Act of 1965.[69]

Previously, to be eligible for a D.C. Tuition Assistance Program scholarship, each applicant had to be a D.C. resident for 12 consecutive months prior to the beginning of the academic year. The applicant also had to begin an undergraduate course of study within 3 years[70] of acquiring a high school diploma or a recognized equivalent of a high school diploma.[71]

Certain requirements of the tuition assistance program remain unchanged. Each applicant must be enrolled in or accepted for enrollment, on at least a half-time basis in a degree program at an eligible institution. Applicants who are currently enrolled must have maintained satisfactory progress in their chosen course of study. Scholarships may only be used for an individual's first undergraduate baccalaureate course of study.

PROGRAM ADMINISTRATION AND FUNDING

The District of Columbia College Access Act of 1999 authorizes appropriations in the amount of $17 million for FY2000 and such sums as may be necessary for 5 succeeding fiscal years, and limits administrative expenses to 7% of annual appropriations. Congress appropriated $17 million for the program for FY2000, specifying that if the program was authorized for a limited number of states, only $11 million would be available.[72] Appropriations were enacted prior to program authorization.

The D.C. Mayor is responsible for administering the D.C. Tuition, Assistance Program, including setting policy and procedures. As enacted, the program allows expansion to public institutions nationwide based on assessment of need for admissions elsewhere, and impact on program costs and consultation with authorizing committees. In May 2000, the Mayor exercised his administrative authority by expanding the program to include

---

[69] 20 U.S.C. 1091 (a)(5).
[70] The 3-year period excludes time served in active military duty, Peace Corps, or Americorps service.
[71] The General Educational Development (GED) test is the most popular form of alternative secondary completion.
[72] Consolidated Appropriations Act (FY2000), P.L. 106-113, November 29, 1999.

public institutions nationwide. Therefore, the full $17 million appropriation was available for the program's first year. For both FY2001 and FY2002 Congress appropriated $17 million for the program.[73] The FY2003 budget request for the program is also $17 million.

P.L. 107-157 also requires the District to establish a dedicated account for the resident tuition program. This dedicated account would contain all future appropriations, any unobligated balances and interest earned on the balances.[74]

The program awarded an average grant of $5,270 to 3,200 applicants in the 2000 school year.[75] Information about the Tuition Assistance Grant Program is available at its website, [http://www.tuitiongrant.washingtondc.gov].

---

[73] District of Columbia Appropriations Act, 2001, P.L. 106-522, November 22, 2000. District of Columbia Appropriations Act, 2002, P.L. 107-96, December 21, 2001.
[74] H.R. 1499 §4.
[75] Hsu, Spencer S. Tuition Plan to Cover All Black Colleges; Senate Votes to Expand D.C. Program. Washington Post, March 16, 2002. p. B1.

Chapter 6

DISTRICT OF COLUMBIA DEPARTMENT OF CORRECTIONS: TRANSFER OF FUNCTIONS TO THE FEDERAL GOVERNMENT

JoAnne O'Bryant

ABSTRACT

On January 14, 1997, President Clinton announced a plan to provide assistance to the District of Columbia's (D.C.) prison system by transferring the D.C. Department of Corrections (DOC) functions to the Federal Bureau of Prisons (FBOP). Part of this initiative became law on August 5, 1997. Under the Balanced Budget Act of 1997, P.L. 105-33, provision is made to alter the authority under which the D.C. Department of Corrections operates. Title XI, Subtitle C, of this act allows the FBOP to take custody of sentenced felons of the District of Columbia through a three-to-five-year transition period. In addition to a federal transition, this change brings an end to a Lorton closure stalemate. For the past two decades, legislation has been introduced regarding the relocation of the D.C. facilities that are in Virginia. Although the Balanced Budget Act of 1997 provided that the Lorton Correctional Complex in Virginia will close by the year 2003, the date of closure was amended in the Taxpayer Relief Act of 1997, P.L. 105-34. The Complex is expected to close by the year 2001.

For approximately 80 years, the D.C. DOC has had facilities in Fairfax County. For the first 65 years, the relationship between the Fairfax County and District of Columbia governments appeared to be amicable and beneficial for Virginia residents. For the last two decades, however, the controversy concerning the facilities in Fairfax County became increasingly intense.

Congressional hearings have documented inadequacies of the facilities at Lorton and poor management of its inmates. Studies, lawsuits, and news stories have cited evidence of D.C. DOC failures. Prison contractual agreements and proposals to close the Virginia facilities have brought mixed reactions from the Fairfax County community and family members of inmates.

Recently, congressional activity has included various hearings to determine the feasibility of transferring the D.C. prison system functions to the federal prison system. Two measures (S. 418 and H.R. 1963) were introduced in the 105th Congress with language to close the D.C. facilities in Virginia. The Clinton Administration also supported a change in the D.C. prison system. A provision in Title XI of the enacted Balanced Budget Act of 1997 federalizes the management of the D.C. corrections system beginning January 1, 2002.

Since the passage of the Balanced Budget Act of 1997, many changes have occurred regarding the federal transition. Provisions in the act addressed to date include D.C. inmate transfers, trustee appointments, land transfer, the truth-in-sentencing commission, and privatization of correctional facilities.

INTRODUCTION

Legislation to relocate the District of Columbia's Lorton Correctional Complex from Fairfax County, Virginia, to another jurisdiction has been introduced repeatedly in Congress for more than two decades. Most of the proposals would have closed the facilities in Virginia and transferred the administrative functions from the Lorton Complex. Thirteen measures affecting the Lorton Complex were introduced from 1975 to 1997. In 1997, an initiative to make adjustments throughout the entire D.C. prison system and transfer functions to the federal prison system gained the support of both the Republican leadership in Congress and the Clinton Administration. In the 1st session of the 105th Congress, a proposal to transfer many responsibilities originally bestowed upon the District of Columbia, including functions within the D.C. prison system, finally became law under the Balanced Budget Act of 1997, P.L. 105-33.

The D.C. Department of Corrections (DOC) has undergone many modifications since the Central Facility was opened in 1916.[76] Administrations have changed, and the inmate population has fluctuated. This chapter provides a brief overview of those adjustments, as well as developments leading up to a federal prison transition, and identifies federal legislation over the past two decades affecting the D.C. DOC.

BACKGROUND

From 1875 to 1910, the District of Columbia had one penal institution for long- and short-term offenders. In 1908, President Theodore Roosevelt appointed a Penal Commission to study overcrowding and conditions in the city jail. The Penal Commission recommended building a workhouse and reformatory facilities in an isolated rural environment. This recommendation was supported by many citizens of the District who opposed the building of a correctional facility in the city because they believed that the existence of a prison would deter economic growth, and that such a facility was inappropriate for the nation's capital. Acting on the recommendations of President Roosevelt's Penal Commission, the 60th Congress appropriated funds to acquire farmland in Occoquan, Virginia, to construct the Lorton Correctional Complex.[77]

For the first 26 years of this century, the responsibility for administering correctional functions was assigned to the Charities and Corrections Committee of the District of Columbia, which was appointed by the District of Columbia Board of Commissioners. In 1926, Congress passed P.L. 69-46; 44 Stat. 209, transferring responsibility for the District of Columbia corrections to the Board of Public Welfare. The board consisted of nine D.C. residents appointed for six-year terms by the commissioners. On June 27, 1946, Congress passed the D.C. Department of Corrections Act, P.L. 79-460, establishing the D.C. Department of Corrections.[78]

---

[76] U.S. Library of Congress, Congressional Research Service, Lorton Reformatory-Establishment, Management and Control, and Jurisdiction to Try Criminals, by the American Law Division, CRS memorandum (Washington: Feb. 6, 1975), p. 3.
[77] Ibid.; D.C. Department of Corrections, Rationale for Locating District of Columbia Correctional Institutions in the State of Virginia (Washington: Dec. 28, 1981); U.S. Library of Congress, Congressional Research Service, History of the Lorton Prison Complex, by Miriam S. Saxon, CRS Report (Washington: June 11, 1975), p. 1.
[78] U.S. Library of Congress, Lorton Reformatory, p. 3.

For approximately 65 years, it appeared that the District and Virginia governments, including Fairfax County officials, had an amicable and mutually beneficial relationship. Virginia officials believed that the existence of the D.C. facilities in Virginia would provide employment opportunities for Virginia residents. The location of the D.C. prison system in Virginia was viewed as an economic plus because the department offered such opportunities and purchased supplies and equipment in Virginia.[79]

These positive attitudes began to change when Virginians drew attention to problems at the Lorton Complex in the late 1960s, and community efforts to move the correctional facilities out of the area began in 1967. A significant number of escapes in the early 1970s triggered fear among residents, and there were calls to transfer D.C. facilities out of Virginia.[80] Virginians cited prison overcrowding, escapes, disturbances, correctional security, illegal drug and prostitution activities, and lawsuits as some of the reasons to move the D.C. facilities out the Fairfax County community. In addition, some community leaders advocated redevelopment of the area where Lorton is presently located.[81]

Congress documented the inadequacies of the facilities at Lorton and poor management of its inmates in hearings and testimony by the General Accounting Office (GAO). In addition, court orders and consent decrees, news stories, and most recently a National Council on Crime and Delinquency (NCCD) report, all cited evidence of Lorton's failures. Since the release of the NCCD report, *District of Columbia Department of Corrections Study, January 1996*, D.C. government officials and other Washington metropolitan area government officials have publicly expressed the need to reduce expenses incurred by the Lorton Complex and other facilities in the Corrections Department.

Presently, the D.C. DOC manages a little over 3,000 inmates in four facilities located in the District of Columbia and on the approximately 3,000 acres of land that contain the Lorton facility. The District is responsible for administering correctional services that are normally operated at a state level. The burden of handling the correctional population in D.C. has strained the city budget. According to the testimony of D.C. DOC officials funding for

---

[79] U.S. Congress, Senate Committee on the Judiciary, Subcommittee on National Penitentiaries, Transfer of Lorton Reformatory to the District of Columbia, hearing, 94th Cong., 1st sess., June 10, July 10, and Sept. 9, 1975 (Washington: GPO, 1975), pp. 47-48.
[80] Ibid., p. 50.
[81] Eric Lipton, "Task Force Suggests Making Lorton Site a Residential Area," Washington Post, June 26, 1997, pp. B1, B7.

correctional services has not kept pace with the population increase and deteriorating facilities.[82] A federal transfer of the D.C. prison system was included in the Balanced Budget Act of 1997, P.L. 105-33, to address the perceived problems in the Corrections Department.

D.C. DEPARTMENT OF CORRECTIONS: DEVELOPMENTS

During the first session of the 105th Congress, there were two major developments affecting the District's Department of Corrections: a proposal to alleviate problems in the D.C. prison system and a Correctional Treatment Facility (CTF) sale/lease-back agreement between the D.C. government and a private prison contractor.

With respect to the first development, the President's National Capital Revitalization and Self Improvement Plan (hereafter called "the President's Plan"), released on January 14, 1997, outlined several proposals to transfer the D.C. prison system to the federal prison system. Some provisions in this initiative became law on August 5, 1997, in the Balanced Budget Act of 1997, P.L. 105-33. According to the President's Plan, the key elements assumed by the federal government in such a transfer would have included the following:

(1) Taking responsibility for sentenced prisoners, appointing a receiver to report to the Control Board, providing funds to construct new facilities and renovate existing facilities, and continuing operation of the Lorton Complex as a prison facility;

(2) Transferring the D.C. DOC responsibility to the Federal Bureau of Prisons (FBOP) over a three-to-five-year period, repairing or expanding the Lorton Complex; and

---

[82] U.S. Congress, House Committee on Government Reform and Oversight, Subcommittee on the District of Columbia, Conditions Within the District of Columbia Department of Corrections, testimony of Margaret Moore, hearing, 104th Cong., 2nd sess., May 22, 1996 (Washington: GPO, 1996), pp. 2-5. And U.S. Congress, House Committee on Appropriations, Subcommittee on the District of Columbia, testimony by Margaret Moore, hearing, 105th Cong., 2nd sess., June 24, 1998, pp. 3-4.

(3) Accepting current prisoners of the D.C. DOC into the FBOP, with new prisoners accepted under federal sentencing standards.

In addition to these responsibilities, the FBOP would have flexibility in transferring inmates throughout the federal prison system, if transfers were needed, to manage the inmate population; the D.C. DOC staff would be required to reapply for positions under federal standards; and the D.C. parole system and community corrections program would become the responsibility of the federal government after the transition period.[83]

At an appropriations hearing for the federal prison system held on April 9, 1997, Director Kathleen Hawk of the FBOP discussed key elements of the President's Plan. If the President's Plan discussed at this hearing had been accepted whole, the D.C. prison transition would have included the renovation of two facilities on the Lorton property and eight new facilities. Two of the new facilities would have been constructed on the Lorton property, and six facilities would have been constructed within 500 miles of Washington, D.C. While new facilities were under construction, D.C. inmates would have been housed in other federal prisons within 500 miles of D.C. Upon completion of the new facilities, the population at the Lorton facilities and the new facilities would have constituted a mixture of D.C. inmates and other new or transferred federal prisoners. Construction cost was estimated at $900 million (to be requested in three increments of $300 million each fiscal year beginning in 1998). Operating costs were estimated at $12 million for FY1999, $20 million for FY2000, and $44 million for FY2001.

Although many of the D.C. corrections provisions in the President's Plan remain in the recently passed law (P.L. 105-33), the law makes one major adjustment pertaining to the construction and renovation proposal outlined above. No facilities will be constructed on the Lorton Complex. Title XI, Subtitle C, of the act requires that no new facilities be constructed on the land and that the Lorton Correctional Complex be closed by the year 2003. The date was later amended to the year 2001 in the Taxpayer Relief Act of 1997 (P.L. 105-34). At the end of the transition period, any property on the Complex will be transferred to the Department of the Interior. The Corrections Trustee will submit funding requests for D.C. Corrections to the

---

[83] U.S. Executive Office of the President, Legislative Affairs Office, The President's National Capital Revitalization and Self-Government Improvement Plan (Washington: Jan. 1997), pp. 4-5.

President and Congress for each fiscal year. These funds will be used to reimburse the Federal Bureau of Prisons for renovation and construction of correctional facilities to house D.C. felons elsewhere.

Since the enactment of the Balanced Budget Act of 1997 in August, several changes have occurred regarding various provisions under Title XI, Subtitle C, Corrections. Activity pertaining to certain sections includes the following:

Felons Sentenced Pursuant to the D.C. Code, Section 11201 (b)

On June 24, 1998, Margaret Moore, the former Director of the D.C. Department of Corrections, testified before the House Committee on Appropriations, Subcommittee on the District of Columbia that 135 female D.C. felons had been transferred to the federal prison system and in January 1998 the Minimum Security Annex had been closed. The Medium Security Facility was also closed after approximately 2,500 D.C. felons were transferred to private sector prison facilities. The Occoquan Workhouse was closed in the summer of 1999. The inmates in the Occoquan facility were transferred to facilities in other states. As of April 6, 2000, approximately 2,300 District of Columbia felons had been transferred into Federal Bureau of Prison (FBOP) custody.

Privatization of Facilities, Section 11201 (c)

According to the Federal Bureau of Prisons (FBOP) *Monday Morning Highlights,* August 11, 1997, the FBOP was preparing for studies to determine the feasibility and cost of privatization efforts for the D.C. prison population. Also, a briefing on prison privatization and the impact on the D.C. prison system was held in the Capitol on September 17, 1997, by the Reason Public Policy Institute. Panel members included representatives from the Florida Correctional Privatization Commission, Wackenhut Corrections, Virginia Department of Corrections, and Corrections Corporation of America. A public hearing regarding potential private prison sites to house D.C. felons was held by site selection officials of the Federal Bureau of Prisons on April 7, 1998.

In the 106th Congress, H.R. 215 (Norton) was introduced to provide discretion to the Director of the Federal Bureau of Prisons in the transfer of D.C. inmates to private contract facilities. The measure was referred to the Committee on Government Reform. At a House Subcommittee on Appropriations, Commerce, Justice, State, the Judiciary, and Related Agencies hearing held on February 24, 1999, the Director of the Federal

Bureau of Prisons, Kathleen Hawk Sawyer testified that the BOP anticipated private contract facilities for low and minimum security beds to be in operation by June 2000. In a more recent hearing before Senate Subcommittee on Criminal Justice Oversight on April 6, 2000, the Director of FBOP testified that although there are nearly 2,300 D.C. felons in facilities operated by or under contract with the FBOP, the agency had delayed efforts to transfer inmates to privately operated facilities due to environmental and legal challenges. In March 2000, however, it was reported that the latest transfer involved 900 D.C. felons who are housed under contract with the State of Virginia.

Land Transfer, Section 11201 (g)(2)
On November 4, 1997, H.R. 2810 (Taylor), was introduced to block the proposed transfer of land now occupied by the Lorton Correctional Complex. The measure was referred to the Committee on Government Reform and Oversight and the Committee on Resources. On September 9, 1998, H.R. 4523 (Davis) was introduced to make amendments to the National Capital Revitalization and Self-Government Improvement Act of 1997 regarding the transfer of land to the General Services Administration. The measure was referred to the Committee on Government Reform and Oversight. In the Consolidated Appropriations Act for FY2000 (P.L. 106-113) a federal payment of $7 million was appropriated for an environmental study and related activities at the Lorton Correctional Complex.

Lorton Correctional Complex, Section 11201 (g)(2)(B)(iii)
Under the Taxpayer Relief Act of 1997, P.L. 105-34, the Lorton Correctional Complex closure date was amended. The Complex is scheduled to close by the year 2001.

Corrections Trustee, Section 11202. U.S. Attorney General Janet Reno appointed former FBOP Assistant Director John L. Clark to be the District of Columbia Corrections Trustee on September 28, 1997. On March 12, 1998, D.C. Corrections Trustee John L. Clark testified before the House Subcommittee on Appropriations for the Departments of Commerce, Justice, State, the Judiciary, and Related Agencies. Mr. Clark discussed his responsibility to provide financial oversight on all aspects of D.C. Department of Corrections. He must also coordinate the transfer of D.C. felons to the federal prison system. The D.C. Corrections Trustee's office was appropriated a federal payment totaling $176 million under the Consolidation Appropriations Act for FY2000 (P.L. 106-113). On March 23,

2000, Mr. Clark testified about FY2001 appropriations for programs before the District of Columbia Subcommittee of the House Appropriations Committee. The Corrections Trustee's request totals $134 million for FY2001.

Truth-in-Sentencing Commission, Section 11211
The following individuals were appointed to the Truth-in-sentencing Commission: Deputy Attorney General Eric Holder (chairman); D.C. Superior Court Judges Harold L. Cushenberry and Frederick H. Weisberg; D.C. Council member Jack Evans; Director of the D.C. Parole Board, Margaret Quick; D.C. Public Defender lawyer, Robert L. Wilkins. Sentencing guidelines recommendations for D.C. felons were completed by the Truth-in-Sentencing Commission on January 31, 1998. Since the D.C. City Council voted to accept recommendations from the D.C. Advisory Commission on Sentencing in 1998, several meetings have taken place regarding sentencing reform in the District of Columbia. The Commission submitted its recommendations to the Council on April 5, 2000. The latest public hearing on sentencing in D.C. was held on May 11, 2000. A restructure of D.C. sentencing guidelines, which must be compliant with federal guidelines, was required by August 5, 2000.

Parole, Section 11231
The U.S. Parole Commission has been responsible for conducting hearings for incarcerated D.C. felons since August 5, 1998. According to the Federal Bureau of Prisons *Monday Morning Highlights,* September 29, 1997, approximately 300 hearings a month are expected during the transition. The U.S. Parole Commission is likely to hire additional parole examiners to accommodate the D.C. felon population, old law federal offenders, military, and new transfer treaty cases. Although the U.S. Parole Commission has been active in making parole release decisions for D.C. felons since 1998, the D.C. Board of Parole has the authority to supervise and revoke parole of D.C. parolees until August 5, 2000. After this date, the D.C. Board of Parole will be abolished and the U.S. Parole Commission will have jurisdiction over all D.C. offenders.

Pretrial Services, Defense Services, Parole, Adult Probation, and Offender Supervision Trustee, Section 11232
On September 28, 1997, U.S. Attorney General Janet Reno appointed the Director of the D.C. Office of Justice Management Institute, John A.

Carver, to be Trustee of the Court Services and Offender Supervision Agency (CSOSA). The agency is responsible for the District of Columbia pretrial, parole and offender supervision services. Mr. Carver testified before the House Committee on Appropriations, Subcommittee on the District of Columbia on June 24, 1998. He discussed his responsibility to transfer D.C. adult supervision programs into a system that meets federal criminal justice standards. According to CSOSA, in the first year, the agency has detained over 600 parole violators. Mr. Carver appeared before the District of Columbia Subcommittee of the House Appropriations Committee on April 28, 1999 to testify about FY2000 appropriations for programs. A federal payment to the D.C. Offender Supervision Trustee's office totaled $58.6 million for Parole Revocation, Adult Probation, and Offender Supervision under the Consolidation Appropriations for FY2000 (P.L. 106-113).

With regard to facility privatization, the D.C. government made an attempt to reduce some expenses within the D.C. DOC, before enactment of P.L. 105-33, by entering into a sale/lease-back agreement with the Corrections Corporation of America (CCA). It is uncertain whether the Southeast D.C.'s Correctional Treatment Facility (CTF) will be part of the FBOP transition, since the facility was sold to the CCA for $52 million, effective March 16, 1997. The agreement between the D.C. government and the CCA is expected to save $70 million in the cost of operating the treatment facility over the life of the contract.[84] In addition, another contractual agreement reached with CCA in May 1997 involved initially sending approximately 900 inmates to Youngstown, Ohio, to alleviate management problems at the Occoquan facility, part of the Lorton Complex. Additional inmates were transferred between August and November of 1997. It was recently reported that nearly 100 inmates were transferred to Youngstown at the beginning of 2000.[85]

POTENTIALLY CONTROVERSIAL ISSUES

Although a transfer of the D.C. prison system to the federal system is expected by the year 2002, several issues and concerns about the D.C. system remain. Most D.C., Virginia, and federal officials support the

---

[84] Cheryl Thompson, "Prison Privatization Called 'Grand Slam' for Change in D.C.," Washington Post, Jan. 31, 1997, sec. B, pp. B1, B6.
[85] Carol D. Leonnig, "Plan to Move Inmates Riles D.C.," Washington Post, July 12, 2000, sec. B, p. B2.

President's Plan and the law (P.L. 105-33) as a means to relieve the District of Columbia of a function and financial burden normally borne by a state. Some citizens and officials in the communities of Fairfax County, Virginia, are supportive because of escapes and disturbances by inmates. However, opponents argue that neither the initial plan by the President nor the current law gives consideration to the communities and families affected by the transition. Some family members of inmates fear that relationships with their loved ones will suffer when the inmates are moved to federal facilities located a long distance away. Many community leaders are recommending that, contrary to recent plans to redevelop the land once the Lorton Correctional Complex is closed, the land stay free of any development indefinitely.[86]

Other controversial transfer issues about the D.C. prison system include: loss of the parole system, since the federal government has abolished parole; the future role of community corrections (e.g., halfway houses, drug treatment); and the use of private-sector contracted facilities outside the jurisdiction of the District of Columbia.

D.C. DEPARTMENT OF CORRECTIONS STRUCTURE

Administration

From 1971 to mid-1997, the Department had at least six Directors and one Acting Director who reported to the Mayor and the City Administrator. Under the statute (P.L. 105-33), the Director of the Department of Corrections was required to report to the D.C. financial control board. The authority was returned to the Mayor in January 1999. A new Director of the D.C. Department of Corrections, Odie Washington, was appointed on March 3, 1999 by the Mayor of the District of Columbia.[87]

---

[86] Eric Lipton, "Leave Lorton Land Open, Fairfax Supervisors Urge," Washington Post, Aug. 5, 1997, Section D, pp. D1, D2.
[87] James Gondles, "District of Columbia Corrections Department," American Correctional Association Directory, 1972-1995 (Lanham, MD: American Correctional Association, 1972-1997).

Staff

Prior to the enactment of a federal transfer, a former D.C. Department of Corrections Director, Margaret Moore, contended that the department was "critically understaffed." She said that the D.C. DOC needed over 400 correctional officers to manage approximately 9,800 inmates. The D.C. DOC employed approximately 3,400 correctional and noncorrectional staff in 1996. The average turnover rate in the D.C. DOC was 10.0% in 1995, compared to an average rate of 12.7% for correctional employees nationwide. During 1995, 197 employees left the agency, including 109 correctional officers.[88] Since the enactment of the Revitalization Act of 1997, the number of staff has been reduced by 32%. As of March 2000, there are 2,141 employees at the D.C. DOC.[89]

Facilities

Parts of the Lorton Correctional Complex are more than 80 years old. Seventy percent of the inmate housing needs to be replaced, and approximately 2,000 new beds need to be built for inmates. Federal prison grant funding match requirements made the financially constrained city unable to apply for such assistance. Under the federal transition, the opportunity to receive funding for prison construction could be restored. To qualify for Truth-in-Sentencing prison construction grants, D.C. officials will have to adjust current laws requiring that inmates serve at least 85% of their imposed sentences.

The first D.C. correctional facilities at Lorton were the Minimum Security Facility, opened in 1910, and the medium security Central Facility, opened in 1916. In 1923, the maximum security facility was constructed, but nearly 40 years elapsed before additional facilities were opened. By 1972, three adult facilities and two youth centers were in operation. In 1999 Lorton had four adult facilities and one youth center. There are two facilities in the District of Columbia. Table 1 lists the facilities and their opening dates.

---

[88] Camille Graham Camp and George M. Camp, "Employee Departures, Resignations, and Retirements," Corrections Yearbook 1996 (South Salem, NY: Criminal Justice Institute, Inc., 1996), pp. 116, 118; Walter Woodward, D.C. Department of Corrections, Communications Division, telephone conversation with public affairs officer, Dec. 1, 1995.

[89] U.S. Congress, House Subcommittee on the District of Columbia, The Office of the Corrections Trustee Fiscal Year 2001 Budget Requests, testimony of John L. Clark, unpublished hearing, 106th Cong., 2nd sess., March 23, 2000.

Table 1. D.C. Department of Corrections Facilities

	Year opened
D.C. Facilities	
Detention Facility (D.C. Jail)	1976
Correctional Treatment Facility	1992
Lorton Facilities	
Minimum Security	1910
Central Facility (medium security)	1916
Maximum Security	1923
Youth Center (medium security)	1960
Medium Security (closed)	1972
Occoquan Facility (closed)	1982
Minimum Security Annex (closed)	1989

Source: D.C. Department of Corrections, Communications Division, and American Correctional Association Directory, District of Columbia Corrections, 1996. p. 68.

Limited inmate correctional industries and educational programs are also administered at Lorton. The Correctional Industries Services (CIS) Division provides opportunities for inmates to work during their incarceration. Although CIS is a popular work program, the amount and type of work for inmates vary in each facility. For example, at the Maximum Security Facility, the only jobs available for inmates are detail (trustee) positions. Few inmates can participate in this type of position. In the Central Facility, more inmates may have an opportunity to work in the farming industry.

Educational Programs

Programs for inmates include various studies at the Lorton Prison College, which operates in conjunction with the University of the District of Columbia. The College, which was developed in 1978, provides courses for inmates in the higher education building located at the Central Facility. Educational services for inmates were threatened to end in the fall of 1997. The future of the educational services remains uncertain, however, the educational and work programs offered in the federal prison system could restore inmate opportunities that are being dropped from the D.C. prison system due to city budget constraints or transitions.

A successful crime prevention program is administered in the Maximum Security Facility. The "Take It from Me" program is a juvenile crime prevention effort that was developed to inform juveniles of the severity of prison life. The inmates in the program provide examples of what they have gone through that led to their incarceration and encourage youth to seek other, positive, goals. Sergeant William Moseley of the D.C. Department of Corrections supervises the inmate participants in the program, which has aided over 9,000 young people since it began in 1993.[90]

Inmate Population

The inmate population at the Complex peaked in March 1995 at 7,022 inmates. By December 1996, the population had declined by 518 (7.4%) to 6,504 inmates. According to the D.C. DOC, the decrease in Lorton's inmate population resulted, in part, from the closing of the medium security Modular Facility. In November 1999, the D.C. DOC supervised approximately 6,080 inmates, most of whom were housed at the Lorton Complex. As of March 2000, it is reported that 2,600 of the inmates are being held at the Complex.[91]

APPENDIX A: CONGRESSIONAL ACTIVITY

Issues regarding the management and location of the D.C. prison facilities are not new. In the 104th Congress, legislation was introduced in both the House and Senate to close the Lorton, Virginia, facility (Lorton Complex) of the D.C. DOC. Congressional inquiry on the closure of the Lorton Complex at an appropriations hearing, however, prompted Kathleen Hawk, Director of the Federal Bureau of Prisons (FBOP), to caution Congress against such action. She urged Congress to have a broader debate on the issue. Hearings on the issue were held by the House Government Reform and Oversight Committee, Subcommittee on the District of Columbia, on March 17 and June 7, 1995. On May 22, 1996, an oversight

---

[90] Sgt. William Moseley, D.C. Department of Corrections, Juvenile Justice Program, prison tour with the program coordinator, July 9, 1997.
[91] U.S. Congress, House Subcommittee on the District of Columbia, The Office of the Corrections Trustee Fiscal Year 2001 Budget Requests, testimony of John L. Clark, unpublished hearing, 106th Cong, 2nd sess, March 23, 2000.

hearing on the D.C. DOC was held before the Subcommittee on the District of Columbia, at which the National Council on Crime and Delinquency (NCCD) released a study on the condition of the Corrections Department. The report made recommendations on improving functions in the D.C. DOC, which included major managerial changes at the Lorton Complex by the year 2001.[92]

In the 105th Congress, both houses passed legislation with language to make changes in the D.C. prison system. On March 10, 1997, S. 418 was introduced in the Senate to close the Lorton Correctional Complex. A similar provision was included in the National Capital Revitalization and Self Improvement Act of 1997 (H.R. 1963), introduced in the House on June 19, 1997. These changes were subsequently signed into law by the President through a balanced budget agreement (P.L. 105-33). Since 1975, legislation has been introduced to close and relocate the Virginia facilities. Numerous hearings have been held to determine the feasibility of closing the Lorton Correctional Complex and transferring the D.C. prison functions to the federal prison system. Appendix B provides a list of legislation introduced between 1975 and 1999.

During the first session of the 105th Congress, several hearings were held to determine the effects of transferring the D.C. prison facility to the federal government. On July 16, 1997, at a hearing held by the Senate Appropriations Committee, Subcommittee on the District of Columbia, the Director of the D.C. Department of Corrections, Margaret Moore, contended that the federal prison system would need to make the same investment that she had requested from Congress for three years. She stated that the D.C. prison system could be improved and remain in its current jurisdiction if adequate resources were provided. Prior to this hearing, the House Subcommittee on Appropriations for the Departments of Commerce, Justice, and State, the Judiciary, and Related Agencies held a hearing on the federal prison system on April 9, 1997. At the hearing, Director Hawk discussed her reasons for changing her opinion, expressed previously, about transferring

---

[92] U.S. Congress, House Committee on Appropriations, Subcommittee on the Departments of Commerce, Justice, and State, the Judiciary, and Related Agencies, hearing, 104th Cong., 1st sess., April 6, 1995 (Washington: GPO, 1995); U.S. Congress, House Committee on Government Reform and Oversight, Subcommittee on the District of Columbia, Closing of Lorton Correctional Complex, hearing on H.R. 461, 104th Cong., 1st sess., Mar. 17 and June 7, 1995 (Washington: GPO, 1995); U.S. Congress, House Committee on Government Reform and Oversight, Subcommittee on the District of Columbia, Conditions Within the District of Columbia Department of Corrections, hearing, 104th Cong., 2nd sess., May 22, 1996 (Washington: GPO, 1996).

the D.C. DOC to the federal prison system. She emphasized a need, in the intervening years, to make the Washington metropolitan area safer, and stated that the federal government should provide some assistance to that end. Director Hawk said that the FBOP could effectively transfer D.C. DOC responsibilities to the federal prison system if sufficient time, resources, and flexibility in management were provided during the transition.[93] The President's Plan and key points of the D.C. prison transfer, as well as an estimated $900 million in construction costs during the first three years of transition, were also discussed during the appropriations hearing. Also, on February 20, 1997, the House Government Reform and Oversight Committee, Subcommittee on the District of Columbia, held a hearing on the President's Plan.

Since the passage of the Balanced Budget Act of 1997, P.L. 105-33, the Director of FBOP, Kathleen Hawk; the D.C. Corrections Trustee, John Clark; and the Director of D.C. Department of Corrections, Margaret Moore, testified at several congressional hearings about the status of the D.C. prison transfer to the federal government.

On March 12, 1998, at a hearing held by the House Subcommittee on Appropriations for the Departments of Commerce, Justice, and State, the Judiciary and Related Agencies, Ms. Hawk discussed how the FBOP was actively evaluating potential sites within 500 miles of the D.C. area for D.C. felons transferred to the federal system. At the same hearing, Mr. Clark testified about his financial oversight responsibilities in the D.C. prison transfer as well as how he must coordinate the transfer of D.C. felons to the federal prison system.

At a hearing before the House Subcommittee on Appropriations, Subcommittee on the District of Columbia on June 24, 1998, Ms. Moore discussed the D.C. prison budget request, the decrease in inmate population, and overall management of the D.C. prison system since the enactment of the law requiring the transfer of D.C. felons to federal prisons. Mr. Clark also testified at this hearing offering similar remarks to those provided in the March 12, 1998 hearing before the House Subcommittee on Appropriations.

On February 24, 1999, at a House Subcommittee on Appropriations for the Department of Commerce, Justice, and State, the Judiciary hearing, the Director of FBOP, discussed the most recent developments regarding the transfer of D.C. inmates to the federal prison system. Some discussion

---

[93] U.S. Dept. of Justice, Federal Bureau of Prisons, Monday Morning Highlights (Washington: Jan. 1997), pp. 1-2.

included the submission of proposals for private contracts to house D.C. inmates. Ms. Hawk testified that the FBOP expected an operational contract for 1,000 beds for minimum security males, Youth Rehabilitation Act (male inmates), and various security levels for female inmates; and 1,200 low security level beds for D.C. inmates by December 1999 and June 2000, respectively. The FBOP announced on April 2, 1999 that the contract for 1,000 beds in Philipsburg, Pennsylvania was awarded to the Cornell Corrections, Inc.

At a House Subcommittee on Appropriations hearing on March 2, 2000 and a Senate Committee on Judiciary, Subcommittee on Criminal Justice Oversight hearing on April 6, 2000, the Director of FBOP testified that due to overcrowding conditions in the federal prison system, it is a challenge to absorb D.C. felons into the federal institutions. She said the change in closure date from the year 2003 to 2001 makes the tasks of accepting the inmates an extraordinary responsibility, although every effort will be made to meet the December 31, 2001 deadline.

APPENDIX B: LEGISLATION ON THE D.C. DEPARTMENT OF CORRECTIONS, 1975-1999 CONGRESS

106th Congress

H.R. 215 (Norton)
District of Columbia Prison Safety Act. Provides discretion to the Director of the Bureau of Prisons in the transfer of District of Columbia inmates to private contract facilities. Introduced January 6, 1999; referred to Committee on Government Reform.

105th Congress

H.R. 4523 (Davis)
Lorton Technical Corrections Act of 1998. Makes technical corrections to the National Capital Revitalization and Self-Government Improvement Act of 1997 regarding the transfer of land to the General Services

Administration. Introduced September 9, 1998; referred to Committee on Government Reform and Oversight.

H.R. 2810 (Taylor)
Directs the Secretary of the Interior to conduct a study to determine the best uses for the property on which the Lorton Correctional Complex is located to obtain the maximum economic benefit from the closure of the Complex under the National Capital Revitalization and Self-Government Improvement Act of 1997. Introduced on November 4, 1997; referred to Committees on Government Reform and Oversight and Resources.

P.L. 105-33, H.R. 2015 (Kasich)
Balanced Budget Act of 1997. Title XI, District of Columbia Revitalization, Subtitle C, refers to the D.C. corrections system, Introduced June 24, 1997; referred to Committee on the Budget. Passed House, June 25, 1997. Passed Senate, June 25. Conference report H.Rept. 105-217 agreed to in House on July 30, 1997; in Senate on July 31, 1997. Signed into law August 5, 1997.

H.R. 1963 (Davis)
National Capital Revitalization and Self-Government Improvement Act of 1997. Title III, Subtitle A, refers to the D.C. corrections system. Introduced June 19, 1997; referred jointly to Committees on Government Reform and Oversight, Ways and Means, and the Judiciary.

S. 418 (Warner)
Would close the Lorton Correctional Complex, to prohibit the incarceration of individuals convicted of felonies under the laws of the District of Columbia in facilities of the District of Columbia Department of Corrections, and for other purposes. Introduced March 10, 1997; referred to Committee on the Judiciary.

104th Congress

H.R. 461 (Wolf)
Would close the Lorton Complex, to prohibit the incarceration of felons under D.C. laws in facilities of the D.C. Department of Corrections, and for other purposes. Introduced January 9, 1995; referred to Committees on Government Reform and Oversight, and Judiciary.

S. 201 (Warner)
Would close the Lorton Complex, to prohibit the incarceration of individuals convicted of felonies under D.C. laws in facilities of the D.C. Department of Corrections. Introduced January 11, 1995; referred to Committee on the Judiciary.

103rd Congress

P.L. 103-322, H.R. 3355
Violent Crime Control and Law Enforcement Act of 1994. Title II, Subtitle D, requires congressional approval of any expansion at Lorton and congressional hearings on future needs. Introduced October 26, 1993; referred to Committee on the Judiciary. Passed House, November 3, 1993. Passed Senate, November 19, 1993. Signed into law, September 13, 1994.

H.R. 3416 (Wolf)
Would establish a commission to consider the closing and relocation of the Lorton Complex. Introduced October 28, 1993; referred to Committees on the Judiciary and the District of Columbia.

H.R. 4293 (Moron)
Would require the transfer of the control of the Lorton Complex to the Bureau of Prisons. Introduced April 21, 1994; referred to Committees on the District of Columbia and the Judiciary.

102nd Congress

H.R. 445 (Wolf)
Would establish the Commission on Closure and Relocation of the Lorton Complex. Introduced January 3, 1991; referred to Committees on the District of Columbia and the Judiciary.

100th Congress

H.R. 5416 (Paris)
Would establish the Congressional Task Force on Concurrent Jurisdiction over Lorton to conduct a study and make recommendations with

regard to the most efficient and effective balance of jurisdictional powers between Virginia and the District of Columbia over the Lorton Complex. Introduced January 28, 1988; referred to Committees on the Judiciary and the District of Columbia.

99th Congress

S. 2019 (Treble)
Would prohibit the District's construction of new facilities, and excessive use of existing facilities, at Lorton Prison in Virginia. Would require the new prison to be in the District. Introduced January 23, 1986; referred to Committee on Governmental Affairs.

H.R. 4050 (Paris)
Would prohibit construction of new D.C. prison facilities, and excessive use of existing facilities, at Lorton. Would require the new prison to be in D.C. Introduced January 23, 1986; referred to Committees on the Judiciary and the District of Columbia.

97th Congress

H.R. 235 (Paris)
Would require the Attorney General to submit to Congress a report prepared by the Federal Bureau of Prisons on the economic and logistic feasibility of moving Lorton Reformatory into the District of Columbia. Introduced January 3, 1983; referred to Committee on the Judiciary.

96th Congress

H.R. 7280 (Paris)
Would require the Attorney General to submit to Congress a report prepared by the Federal Bureau of Prisons on the economic and logistic feasibility of moving Lorton Reformatory into the District of Columbia. Introduced October 1, 1982; referred to Committee on the Judiciary.

94th Congress

S. 1243 (Scott)
Would require the Attorney General to assume responsibility for the erection of correctional facilities within the District if such facilities have not been provided by January 1, 1978. Authorizes the Attorney General to dispose of all federally owned lands in the Lorton-Occoquan area of Fairfax County, Virginia, that are managed by the District as soon as possible after January 1, 1978. Introduced March 19, 1975; referred to Committee on the Judiciary.

Chapter 7

DISTRICT OF COLUMBIA MANAGEMENT RESTORATION ACT OF 1999: A FACT SHEET

Eugene Boyd

ABSTRACT

H.R. 433, the District of Columbia Management Restoration Act of 1999, would repeal the District of Columbia Management Reform Act of 1997 (Subtitle B of Title XI of the Balanced Budget Act of 1997, P.L. 105-33). By repealing Subtitle B, the bill would transfer to the Mayor of the District of Columbia management authority for the daily operations of the city's nine largest departments. This transfer in management authority would represent significant progress by the city's elected government, working with the District of Columbia's Financial Responsibility and Management Assistance Authority, in its effort to restore self-government largely lost since April 1995. Supporters of the transfer, including the mayor, argue that the transfer of authority would lead to greater accountability and less diffusion of responsibility by clarifying the lines of authority between the mayor and the Authority. Opponents may counter that the transfer is premature, arguing that the goals of the District of Columbia Management Reform Act of 1997 and the District of Columbia Financial Responsibility and Management Assistance Act have not yet been fully realized.

BACKGROUND

On April 17, 1995, President Clinton signed the District of Columbia Financial Responsibility and Management Assistance Act, P.L. 104-8, creating the District of Columbia's Financial Responsibility and Management Assistance Authority. The Authority is given broad powers and extensive control over the operations of a city government faced with growing debt, budget deficits, cash shortfalls, deteriorating city services, and management inefficiencies. Its mission is to eliminate the District's budget deficits and cash shortages and to assist the District in restructuring and reforming the delivery of city services. The Act creating the Authority required that the District of Columbia produce four consecutive balanced budgets before the Authority could return power to the elected city officials. The creation of the Authority reduced the role of elected city leaders – the mayor and city council – in the operation of city government.

In 1997, the mayor's authority over daily operations of the city government was further reduced with the passage of the District of Columbia Management Reform Act of 1997 (Subtitle B of title XI of the Balanced Budget Act of 1997, P.L. 105-33). The Act explicitly transferred to the Authority control of the city's nine largest agencies: the Department of Administrative Services; the Department of Consumer and Regulatory Affairs; the Department of Corrections; the Department of Employment Services; the Department of Fire and Emergency Medical Services; the Department of Housing and Community Development; the Department of Human Services; the Department of Public Works; and the Department of Public Health. It gave the Authority the power to appoint and dismiss agency heads; and created the position of Chief Management Officer, with responsibility for the day-to-day operations of the city government and the development of long range management reform plans. Most significantly, the transfer of power to appoint and dismiss agency heads and implement management reforms represented a major restructuring of the Authority's relationship with the mayor and the city council. To many city residents it was evidence of the further diminished self-government and the city's home rule charter.

ANALYSIS

Since the passage of the Management Reform Act of 1997, the elected leadership of the city government and the Authority have changed. There are four new members of the Authority. In November 1998, the city elected a new mayor and three new council members, all of whom ran as reform candidates. The new mayor, Anthony Williams, the city's former chief financial officer, has been given partial credit for the city's financial turn-around. During his tenure, under the guidance of the Authority, the city produced two budgets with surpluses, including a $450 million surplus for 1998.

Since his election, Mayor Williams has lobbied for return of management authority over the nine departments previously under the jurisdiction of the city's chief management officer, who has since departed. He has been supported in this effort by the Authority. The Authority, the mayor, and the council have pledged to work together in an effort to improve city services and return self-government to the District.

Sponsors of H.R. 433, the District of Columbia Management Restoration Act of 1999, include Delegate Norton (D-D.C.); Representative Morella (R-Md.); and Representative Davis (R-Va.), the Chairman of the Subcommittee on the District of Columbia of the House Government Reform Committee. The measure also has the support of the Authority. The bill was approved by the House Government Reform Committee on February 3, 1999. The bill's sponsors believe that significant progress has been made in returning the city to financial solvency and in implementing management reforms. The bill states that additional progress could be made by more clearly defining the roles of the Authority and elected officials, and by reducing redundancy and confusion about accountability and authority. Supporters hope that these political changes, coupled with two years of consecutive budget surpluses, will convince Congress to repeal the Management Reform Act of 1997. Opponents may counter that despite this recent period of cooperation between the Authority and elected officials, repeal of the Management Reform Act is premature.

Chapter 8

DISTRICT OF COLUMBIA APPROPRIATIONS ACT FOR FY2003: COMPARISON OF GENERAL PROVISIONS OF P.L. 107-96 AND S. 2809

Eugene Boyd

ABSTRACT

On September 17, 2002, the District's Chief Financial Officer (CFO) notified city leaders of the potential $323 million budget shortfall facing the city in FY2003. On July 26, 2002, the Senate Appropriations Committee reported S. 2809, a bill appropriating funds for the District of Columbia for FY2003, and the Senate report (S. Report 107-225) accompanying the bill. In keeping with last year's efforts, which reduced the number of general provisions from 67 to 41, S. 2809, as reported by the Committee, reduces the number of general provisions from 41 to 36. It modifies a number of provisions that some observers consider intrusive. Among the more controversial sections is a general provision that prior to FY2002, prohibited the use of both federal and District funds to implement a 1992 District law allowing unmarried heterosexual or homosexual couples to register as domestic partners. Under the provision, first enacted as part of the District's FY2002 appropriations act, and included in S. 2809, District employees who register as domestic partners would be allowed to include domestic partners under their health insurance policies. The provision lifts the ban on the use of District, but not federal, funds to implement the 1992 Health Care Benefits Expansion Act.

The District's elected leadership has voiced concern about the inclusion of social riders in past appropriations bills and hope to negotiate with the congressional leaders on the contents of the general provisions to be included in the FY2003 appropriations bill for the District of Columbia. In previous years, city officials had complained about the inclusion of a number of home rule and "social" riders dealing with such issues as voting representation in Congress, abortion, medical marijuana, domestic partners health insurance expansion, and needle and syringe exchange programs.

The District of Columbia Appropriations Act for FY2003, as reported by the Senate Appropriations Committee, would continue existing prohibitions and restrictions on the use of federal and District funds for abortions and medical marijuana. However, S. 2809 includes provisions that would remove existing restrictions on the use of District funds for needle exchange programs, statehood lobbying, court challenges aimed at providing city residents with voting representation in Congress. It also includes a provision that would allow the District to continue to use local funds to administer the city's Health Care Benefits Expansion Act of 1992, as described earlier in this summary.

BACKGROUND

The chronology of District of Columbia Appropriations for FY2003 is as outlined below. On February 4, 2002, President Bush submitted his budget recommendations for FY2003. The Administration's proposed budget included $379 million in federal payments and assistance to the District of Columbia. On May 25, 2002, Mayor Anthony Williams, transmitted to Congress a budget approved by the city council that totaled $7.3 billion in operating funds and capital outlays, including $5.7 billion in general operating fund expenditures; $662 million in enterprise funds; and $931 million in capital outlays. The District budget, which must be approved by Congress, requests $698.4 million in special federal payments for courts, corrections, and other activities. On July 26, 2002, the Senate Appropriations Committee reported S. 2809, the Senate version of the District of Columbia Appropriations Act for FY2003. The Senate Appropriations Committee recommends an appropriation of $517 million in special federal assistance to the District of Columbia, including $15 million for emergency and security management. This is $138 million more than the $379 million requested by the Administration. On September 17, 2002, the city's CFO released official financial projections showing a potential deficit of $323 million for FY2003.

Congress set an October 1, 2002, deadline for the city to develop a plan of action on the deficit, which may include a combination of tax increases, budget cuts, and the use of reserve funds.

Differences exist between the general provisions of S. 2809 and those of the District of Columbia Appropriations Act for FY2002, P.L. 107-96. The Senate Appropriation bill continues a trend established by last year's appropriations act, which included 25 fewer general provisions; 41 down from 67 in the FY2001 appropriations. This year's Senate Appropriations Committee version of bill includes 5 fewer provisions and provides for expanded local autonomy. It would continue to allow the District to use its funds to implement the city's Health Care Benefits Expansion Act (this provision was first approved in the FY2002 appropriations act), and removes penalties for teenage smoking, restrictions on the use of District funds for needle exchange programs, and provisions limiting city involvement in court challenges aimed at providing city residents with voting representation in Congress. The Act maintains prohibitions and restrictions on the use of federal and District funds for abortions, except in cases of rape or incest; and medical marijuana.

In previous years, city officials had complained to past Administrations and the leadership of Congress about the inclusion of a number of social riders dealing with such issues as abortion, medical marijuana, domestic partners health insurance expansion, and needle and syringe exchange programs. They asserted that such riders interfered with the right of District residents to make their own policy decisions, and violated the spirit of home rule. Proponents of social riders counter that such provisions are within the powers of Congress under Article 1, Section 8, of the Constitution, which conveys to Congress exclusive legislative control over the District of Columbia. In addition, supporters of specific social riders, such as the prohibition against the implementation of the District's domestic partners health care expansion program, contend that they are intended to protect the institution of marriage, or, in the case of medical marijuana and needle exchange programs, prohibit government sanctioning of illegal drug use.

The following is a side-by-side comparison of the general provisions of the District of Columbia Appropriations Act for FY2003, P.L. 107-96, and the Senate bill S 2809. House and conference provisions will be added when the legislation is reported out of the respective committee. This comparison follows the structure of P.L 107-96. Any identical or equivalent Senate language that may not share the same section number as corresponding P.L. 107-96 provisions is identified in the same row as its P.L. 107-96 counterpart.

DISTRICT OF COLUMBIA GENERAL PROVISIONS: P.L. 107-96 AND S. 2809

P.L. 107-96	S. 2809	House	Conference
Sec. 101. *Prohibition Against Deficit Spending.* The provision prohibits deficit spending by limiting spending to not more than the amount specifically appropriated.	Sec. 101. Identical to provision in P.L. 107-96.		
Sec. 102. *Payment of Travel and Dues Related Expenses.* The provision allows funds appropriated under this Act to be used for travel and dues-related expenses of organizations concerned with the work of the District when approved by the mayor, and by the chair of the city council in the case of travel and dues related to the activities of the city council.	Sec. 102. Identical to provision in P.L. 107-96.		
Sec. 103. *Payment of Judgments.* The provision allows District funds to be used to by judgments against the city. The provision does not affect or modify Sec. 11(c) Title XII of the District of Columbia Income and Franchise Tax Act of 1947 D.C. Code, sec. 47-1812.11(c)(3), a provision governing credits and refunds for underpayments of District taxes.	Sec. 103. Identical to provision in P.L. 107-96.		
Sec. 104. *Prohibition Against the Carryover of Appropriated Funds.* The provision requires the city to expend funds appropriated for FY2002 during that fiscal year, unless provided by another provision of this act.	Sec. 104. FY2003 language identical to provision in P.L. 107-96.		
Sec. 105. *Use of Public Schools.* The act allows public schools to be used for community or partisan political activities during non-school hours.	Sec. 105. Identical to provision in P.L. 107-96.		
Sec. 106. *Congressional Inspection of Personnel Records.* The personnel records of all persons employed by the District government would be made available for inspection by House and Senate authorization and appropriations subcommittees, and the District of Columbia City council.	Sec. 106. Identical to provision in P.L. 107-96.		

P.L. 107-96	S. 2809	House	Conference
Sec. 107. *Prohibition on the Use of Funds for Lobbying*. Prohibits the city from spending city or federal funds to defeat any legislation pending before Congress or any -- state legislature. Allows the use of District funds for lobbying except in instances involving the promotion or support of any boycott or activities in support of statehood for the District or voting representation in Congress. See Sec. 124.	Sec. 109. Identical to provision in P.L. 107-96.		
Sec. 108. *Capital Borrowing Plan*. Requires the mayor to develop an annual capital outlays borrowing plan. The plan is to include quarterly and project information. The mayor is to report to the city council and Congress on actual and projected spending.	Sec. 108. Identical to provision in P.L. 107-96.		
Sec. 109. *Prohibition on the Reprogramming of Funds*. Prohibits the District government from reprogramming federal and District funds appropriated under the act for seven specific activities. Funds could not be reprogrammed in order to: — create new programs; — eliminate a program or project; — establish or change allocations specifically denied, limited, or increased by Congress; — increase funds for activities or personnel in areas where funds have been denied or restricted; — re-establish funding for any project previously deferred through reprogramming; — augment existing programs or projects by reprogramming funds that exceed $1 million or 10% of the existing program's funding;	Sec. 109. Identical to provision in P.L. 107-96.		

P.L. 107-96	S. 2809	House	Conference
— prohibit a 20% or greater increase in personnel assigned to a specific project. Funds may be reprogrammed after congressional review by House and Senate appropriations Committees. Limits the transfer of reprogrammed funds to not more than 2% of the local funds in the appropriations.			
Sec. 110. *Limitation on the Use of Appropriated Funds.* Limits the use of funds to the activities or objects for which the appropriations were made except as otherwise provided by law.	Sec. 110. Identical to provision in P.L. 107-96.		
Sec. 111. *Merit Personnel Act Responsibility of the Mayor.* States that the mayor shall be responsible for the administration of personnel function of employees under the city's merit pay personnel code. In determining employee compensation, the provisions of the District of Columbia Government Comprehensive Merit Personnel act of 1978 shall apply.	Sec. 111. Identical to provision in P.L. 107-96.		
Sec. 112. *City Council Review of Revised Revenue Estimates.* Requires the mayor to submit to the City council revised revenue estimates for the first quarter of FY2002 not later than 30 days after the first quarter of FY2002.	Sec. 112. *City Council Review of Revised Revenue Estimates.* Requires the mayor to submit to the City council revised revenue estimates for the first quarter of FY2003 not later than 30 days after the first quarter of FY2003.		
Sec. 113. *Sole Source Contracts.* Prohibits sole source contracts for services unless competitive bidding is not feasible and the contract has been approved by the control board as set forth by D.C. Code, sec. 1-1183.3.	Sec. 113. Identical to provision in P.L. 107-96.		
Sec. 114. *Sequestration under the Balanced Budget.* In order to comply with sequestration order under Balanced Budget	Sec. 114. Identical to provision in P.L. 107-96.		

P.L. 107-96	S. 2809	House	Conference

and Emergency Deficit Control Act of 1985, federal funds appropriated under a District of Columbia appropriations act are to be sequestered from each account and not the aggregate total of those accounts.

Sec. 115. *Gifts and Donations.* Allows District government agencies and officials accept gifts and donations in FY2000 only if:

- the mayor approves, (this provision does not apply in cases of gifts or donation to the city council);
- the gift or donation is used to carry out an agency function;
- the government entity receiving the gift or donation keeps records of all gifts and donations available for audit and public inspection.

This section does not apply to the Board of Education.

Sec. 116. *Prohibits the Use of Funds for Statehood Lobbying.* Prohibits the use of federal funds for the payment of expenses related to the offices of U.S. Senate or U.S. House of Representative under the District of Columbia Statehood Constitution initiative.

Sec. 117. *Abortion.* Prohibits the use of funds for abortion services except in cases of rape, incest, or when the mother's health is endangered.

Sec. 118. *Health Care Benefits Expansion Act.* Prohibits the use of federal funds to implement the Health Care Benefits Expansion Act of 1992, which extends medical, employment, and government benefits to unmarried couples, including homosexuals.

	Sec. 115. Identical to provision in P.L. 107-96.		
	Sec. 116. Identical to provision in P.L. 107-96.		
	Sec. 117. Identical to provision in P.L. 107-96.		
	Sec. 118. Identical to provision in P.L. 107-96, which prohibits the use of federal funds, but allows the use of District funds.		

P.L. 107-96	S. 2809	House	Conference
Sec. 119(a). *Acceptance of Grant Funds Not Included in Ceiling.* The mayor, after consulting with the CFO, may accept and expend grants from private and federal sources that are not part of this appropriation. Such gifts may be accepted and expended only after the CFO has submitted to the city council a detailed report regarding such grants. The city council has 14 days after receipt of the report to review and approve its acceptance or to file a resolution of disapproval. The Council has 30 calendar days from initial receipt of the report from the CFO to act on a resolution of disapproval. The provision: — prohibits the city from expending city funds in anticipation of a grant award; — requires the CFO to submit to the city council and House and Senate Appropriations Committees detailed reports regarding all federal and private grants approved under this section.	Sec. 119. Identical to provision in P.L. 107-96.		
Sec. 120. *Use of City Vehicles.* Limits a District employee's use of official vehicles only to performance of official duties. Grants four exceptions: — a police officer may use police vehicles to travel to and from work and home only if the officer resides in the District of Columbia, or is granted permission by the Chief of Police; — an employee of the Fire and Emergency Ambulance Department who resides in the District and is on call 24 hours a day; — the mayor; and — chair of the city council.	Sec. 120. Identical to provision in P.L. 107-96 except inventory of all vehicles owned, leased or operated by the city is due November 15, 2002.		

P.L. 107-96	S. 2809	House	Conference
Requires the CFO to submit an inventory of all vehicles owned, leased or operated by the District government by November 15, 2001. Does not specify to whom the inventory is to be submitted. Includes an additional provision that requires the district to conduct a cost analysis for the procurement of all goods and services in excess of $2,500, excluding goods and services being acquired by CIO, CFO, and Metropolitan Police. In conducting such analysis the District is to compare costs under District procurement regulations and procedures with those applicable under 1e federal GSA supply schedules.			
Sec. 121. *Special Education Evaluation Time Frame.* This provision requires that the school board complete an evaluation of students who may be in need of special education services within 120 days of the student's referral, and to place students with special education needs, as defined by federal law (Individuals with Disabilities education Act (20 U.S.C. 1401 (a)(l)) or the Rehabilitation Act of 1973 29 U.S.C. 1406(8)) in appropriate programs.	Sec. 121. Identical to provision in P.L. 107-96.		
Sec. 122. *Buy American Act.* Encourages District government to comply with the (Buy American Act 41 U.S.C. 10a-10c). Includes a sense of the Congress provision encouraging the purchase of American made products.	Sec. 122. Identical to provision in P.L. 107-96.		
Sec. 123. *Inspector General Audits.* Only the District of Columbia Inspector general may conduct and certify agency audits in compliance with the District of Columbia Procurement Practices Act of 1985 (D.C. Code, sec. 1-1182.8(a)(4).	Sec. 123. Identical to provision in P.L. 107-96.		

P.L. 107-96	S. 2809	House	Conference
Sec. 124. *Voting Representation Cost Prohibition.* Prohibits the use of federal and district funds, including funds for the corporation counsel, to cover the cost of court challenges aimed at providing city residents with voting representation in Congress.	Sec. 124. Voting Representation Cost Prohibition. Prohibits the use of federal, but not District, funds to cover the cost of court challenges aimed at providing city residents with voting representation in Congress.		
Sec. 125. *Needle Exchange Program.* Prohibits the creation and funding of a needle change program with federal or District government funds. Such programs may be funded with private funds and must be accounted for separately.	Sec. 125. Needle Exchange Program. Allows the use of District funds for such programs, but prohibits the use of federal government funds. Requires entities administering needle exchange programs to track program funds used for such activities separately from any funds appropriated under this act.		
Sec. 126. *CFO Certifications.* Funds may not be used to pay agency CFOs 60 days after the passage of this Act if the agency CFO has not filed a statement with the Mayor and CFO of the District certifying that the agency CFO understands and will abide by the duties and restrictions of his office.	Sec. 126. Identical to provision in P.L. 107-96.		
Sec. 127. *Medical Marijuana Initiative.* Prohibits the use of federal or District funds in carrying out any law or regulation that legalizes or reduces the penalty for session of a Schedule I substance, including the medical use of marijuana. Prohibits the implementation of citizen approved medical marijuana initiative.	Sec. 127. Identical to provision in P.L. 107-96.		
Sec. 128. *Conscience Clause Covering Contraceptive Coverage in Private Health Plans.* The provision requires the inclusion of a conscience clause allowing employers to exclude contraceptive coverage in the employer's health insurance plan for moral or religious reasons.	Sec. 128. Identical to provision in P.L. 107-96.		

	P.L. 107-96	S. 2809	House	Conference
Sec. 129.	*Prompt Payment of Appointed Counsel.* Requires the DC Court of appeals to make payment to counsel representing indigent persons, and children in neglect and abuse cases within 45 days of receiving a payment voucher. Failure to make payment within the 45-day time period would require the DC Court of appeals to pay interest to the attorneys representing indigent persons, and children in neglect and abuse cases. Requires the Court to establish standards for the submission of completed vouchers. Covers claims received during fiscal year 2002 and unpaid claims that remained at the end of fiscal year 2001.	Sec. 129. Covers claims received during fiscal year 2003 and unpaid claims that remained at the end of fiscal year 2002.		
Sec. 130.*	*Teenage Smoking.* Bans possession of tobacco by minors and imposes fines, community service, and revocation of driving privileges. Provides $100,000 federal assistance for enforcement activities.	Not included in this bill.		
Sec. 131.	*Budget-linked Quality of Life Factors.* Identifies a number of quality-of-life indicators that characterize the city's deficiencies in the areas of crime, education, corrections, management of public services. Directs the mayor to submit quarterly reports to House and Senate appropriation and oversight committees.	Sec. 131. Identical to Sec. 131 of P.L. 107-96.		
Sec. 132.	*Corporation Counsel Review of Private Lawsuits.* The provision permits the district's corporation counsel to review and comment on briefs in lawsuits filed by private citizens, and to consult government officials regarding such lawsuits. This includes lawsuits seeking voting representation in Congress.	Sec. 131. Identical to Sec. 132 of P.L. 107-96.		
Sec. 133.*	*Emergency Cash Reserve and Contingency Reserve Funds.* Requires budget reserve of $120 million in FY2002,	Not included in this bill.		

P.L. 107-96	S. 2809	House	Conference
and $70 million in FY2003. For each of fiscal years 2004 and 2005 the District must maintain a cumulative cash reserve of 150 million. Outlines the conditions under which budget and cash reserves may be budgeted to include: – CFO certification that funds are available; – amounts are to be obligated or expended in accordance with laws enacted by city council; – prohibition on the use of funds for agencies under court ordered receivership; and – only after House and Senate Appropriations Committees have been notified by the mayor in writing 30 days in advance of any obligation or expenditure. Requires funds taken from the reserve be replenished in order to maintain required balance. Transfers all funds in the $150 million budget reserve created under Sec. 6-113 into the Emergency and Contingency Reserve Funds established under Sec. 9 of P.L. 106-522.			
Sec. 134.* *Integrated Products Team.* Prohibits the appropriation of funds for the integrated Product Team. The city has approved a reorganization plan for the team and a Capital Construction services Administration.	Not included in this bill.		
Sec. 135. *Revised Operating Budget Submission.* Requires the CFO to submit to appropriate committees of Congress, the mayor, and the city council a revised appropriated funds operating budget no later that 30 days after the enactment of this act. The revised budget should reflect anticipated actual expenditures for the fiscal year.	Sec. 132. Identical to Sec. 135 of P.L. 107-96		
Sec. 136.* *City Council Chairman Compensation.* Eliminates the provision that provides $10,000 in additional annual	Not included in this bill.		

P.L. 107-96	S. 2809	House	Conference
compensation to the chairman of the city council above the amount of compensation provided to other council members. Provides additional compensation to chairman of the city council residual to $10,000 less than the compensation paid to the mayor.			
Sec. 137. *Risk Management of Settlements and Judgments.* Allows any district government agency to pay a settlement or judgement stemming from claim or lawsuit that does not exceed $10,000.	Sec. 133. Identical to Sec. 137 of P.L. 107-96.		
Sec. 138.* *Closing of Certain Streets.* Waives the period of congressional review for closing of portions of 2nd and N Streets, NE.	Not included in this bill.		
Sec. 139 *Boy Scouts.* Prohibits the use of District or federal funds for payment to plaintiffs awarded $50,000 by the District's Commission on Human Rights related to Boy Scout's policy prohibiting homosexuals from serving as scout leaders.	Sec. 134. Identical to Sec. 139 of P.L. 107-96.		
Sec. 140.* *Attorney's Fees for Special Education.* Prohibits the use funds appropriated under this and subsequent appropriation acts from being used to pay attorney's associated with representing disabled students fees incurred prior to the enactment of this act. Requires the DC public school system to submit to Congress a report that lists all judgments against the DC public schools under the Individuals with Disabilities Education Act (IDEA). The report is to be submitted within 60 days of enactment of this act and is to include detailed information for each of the years 1999 to 2001, on the amount paid and owed plaintiffs' attorneys, and attorneys representing the school board.	Not included in this bill.		

P.L. 107-96	S. 2809	House	Conference
Sec. 141.* *GAO Report on Attorney's Fees for Special Needs Students*. Directs GAO, with the assistance of relevant agencies and House and Senate subcommittees on DC appropriations and oversight, to submit by March 31, 2002, a report to the House and Senate appropriations and oversight committees detailing the awards in judgment rendered in the District of Columbia that were in excess of the cap imposed by prior appropriations acts in effect during the fiscal year when the work actions brought against the District of Columbia Public Schools under the individuals with Disabilities Education Act (20 U.S.C. § 1400 et. seq.).	Not included in this bill.		

* Provisions included in P.L 107-96, but not included in S. 2809.

Chapter 9

DISTRICT OF COLUMBIA TERRORISM RESPONSE

Eugene Boyd and Michael Fauntroy

INTRODUCTION

As the nation's capital, the District of Columbia is likely to be a prime target for terrorist attacks. The general assessment among local and federal officials involved in disaster response planning for the capital is that the District of Columbia government provided an inadequate response to the emergency conditions following the September 11, 2001, terrorist attacks. District officials acknowledged some problems, but insist that an emergency response plan was executed in a timely manner. Members of Congress have called for an assessment of preparation in D.C. for future attacks to ensure an adequate response in the event of future terrorist attacks so as to prevent the loss of life and maintain the continuity of federal and District government functions.

CURRENT SITUATION

D.C. Plan

The District government has prepared a "Family Preparedness Guide," an eight-page document that outlines steps individuals and businesses should take before, during, and after an emergency. Pre-emergency, the guide discusses ways in which families can create an emergency plan; prepare an emergency kit to take wherever necessary; and pet care. After an emergency strikes, the guide describes what one can do if the power goes out; dealing with technological hazards and natural hazards; what to do to ensure one has clean water; and how to recover from an emergency. The guide also provides a list of emergency District telephone numbers. Internet web sites are also provided so that additional information can be accessed. The *District's Emergency Management Agency (EMA) web site* provides a link to the guide.

POLICY ANALYSIS

One of the primary problems in emergency planning in the District appears to be communication coordination. In the wake of the September 11, 2001 attack, there have been numerous reports of poor communication among District officials and District officials and regional and federal authorities. In addition, District officials acknowledged that insufficient notification was provided to local residents and workers regarding steps to be taken in response to the crisis. There is a history to this problem: the same difficulty was cited during hearings after an Air Florida passenger jet crash into the 14th Street Bridge during a 1982 blizzard.

The city's lack of a detailed response plan for terrorism attacks arguably contributed to delays in evacuating affected parts of the city and, if there had been more casualties, could have hampered medical care. As the events of September 11 unfolded, the city's police command improvised, putting together response elements from past events. The police chief activated the civil disturbance unit, which had been used during the World Bank and IMF meetings last year; called in all off-duty officers, as is the custom for presidential inaugurations, and implemented a traffic plan developed for Y2K.

The District's new plan noted above is aimed at responding to and preventing the reported failures of District officials during the early stages of the events of September 11, 2001. Among the reported failures were the following:

- The city's emergency broadcast system was never activated.
- Satellite telephones necessary for using a backup communications system were never delivered to top city leaders.
- An email message from the mayor's chief of staff to District of Columbia government employees that ordered them to evacuate was countermanded by a later email message from the city administrator.
- The District's health department was unable to monitor radio networks used by hospitals, thereby rendering the agency unable to determine hospital bed availability.
- The Metropolitan Police Department does not have an antiterrorism strategy, or guidelines telling officers and staff how and where to respond.

These reported failures can be used as yardsticks to help determine District readiness in the event of a future attack.

Lead city officials, including the police and fire chiefs, the director of emergency management, and the deputy mayor for public safety, defended the city's response to the crisis during an appearance on a local radio show. The *broadcast* can be assessed from the city's police web site.

ROLE OF CONGRESS/LEGISLATION

The House Appropriations Committee, during its September 20, 2001 markup of the District of Columbia Appropriations Act for FY2002, approved an amendment to reprogram $16 million in funds intended to cover the city's costs of providing security for a planned – but now cancelled – September meeting of the World Bank and International Monetary Fund. The Committee's bill allocates the $16 million for emergency security plans for the city. Further, it withholds half the $16 million pending the submission of emergency security plans by the city to the appropriate federal authorities.

The FY2002 Department of Defense appropriations included $200,000,000 in emergency preparedness funds. Table 1 lists how the funds are to be earmarked.

Table 1: 2002 District of Columbia Emergency Preparedness Appropriations

Item	Amount Appropriated (in US$)
Protective Clothing and Breathing Apparatus	7,144,000
Specialized Hazardous Materials Equipment	1,032,000
Chemical and Biological Weapons Preparedness	10,355,000
Pharmaceuticals for Responders	2,100,000
Response and Communications Capability	14,960,000
Search, Rescue, and other Emergency Equipment and Support	8,850,000
Equipment, Supplies, and Vehicles for the Office of the Chief Medical Examiner	1,780,000
Hospital Containment Facilities for the Department of Health	8,000,000
Office of the Chief Technology Officer Communications Systems	45,494,000
Emergency Traffic Management	20,700,000
Training and Planning	9,949,000
Increased Facility Security	25,536,000
Washington Metropolitan Area Transit Authority	39,100,000
Metropolitan Washington Council of Governments	5,000,000
Total	**200,000,000**

Source: Conference Report for *H.R. 3338*. FY2002 Department of Defense Appropriations.

INDEX

#

10 square miles, 6

A

abortion, 94, 95, 99
abortions, 94, 95
accountability, 55, 89, 91
al Qaeda, 4
Alaska, 11, 27
Alexandria, 6, 7, 8, 34
Alexandria County, 6, 8
amendments, 19, 27, 74
Andrew Ellicott, 1, 3
annual appropriation, 64
Arlington County, 6, 34
Armed Services, 17

B

Balanced Budget Act, 50, 67, 68, 71, 73, 82, 84, 89, 90
BEE, 57, 58, 60
Benjamin Banneker, 1, 3
Board of Education, 9, 43, 44, 45, 47, 48, 53, 54, 55, 56, 57, 58, 62, 99
Board of Elections and Ethics
 BEE, 57

Budget, 50, 67, 68, 71, 73, 78, 80, 82, 84, 89, 90, 98, 104
budget deficits, 90
Bush, 94

C

candidates, 47, 58
Capability, 110
capital outlays, 94, 97
cash shortfalls, 90
CCA, 76
CFO, 93, 94, 100, 102, 103, 104
Charles Dickens, 3
charter schools, 43, 44, 45, 50, 51
Chief Financial Officer
 CFO, 10, 93
Christopher Columbus, 3, 12
CIS, 79
city council, 6, 25, 44, 48, 50, 54, 56, 57, 58, 62, 90, 94, 96, 97, 99, 100, 103, 104
city services, 90, 91
civil rights, 46, 50
Civil War, 3
Clinton, 10, 67, 68, 90
Clinton Administration, 68
College Access Improvement Act, 63, 64

Committee of the Whole, 17, 21, 23, 24, 39
Committee on Banking, Finance and Urban Affairs, 18
compliance, 101
Congress, 1, 2, 3, 4, 5, 6, 7, 8, 9, 10, 13, 14, 15, 16, 17, 18, 19, 20, 21, 23, 24, 25, 26, 27, 28, 29, 30, 31, 32, 33, 35, 36, 37, 38, 39, 40, 43, 44, 45, 47, 48, 49, 51, 52, 58, 59, 61, 62, 63, 65, 66, 68, 69, 70, 71, 73, 78, 80, 81, 83, 84, 85, 86, 87, 91, 94, 95, 97, 101, 102, 103, 104, 105, 109
congressional activity, 68
congressional consideration, 2
congressional leaders, 94
Congressional Record, 27, 40
Connogocheague Creek, 7
constitutionality, 18
correctional facilities, 68, 70, 73, 78, 87
Correctional Industries Services CIS, 79
Correctional Treatment Facility CTF, 71, 76, 79
Corrections Corporation of America CCA, 73, 76
Court Services and Offender Supervision Agency CSOSA, 76
CSOSA, 76
CTF, 71, 76

D

DCBE, 44
DCPS, 49, 50, 51, 53
Delegate to Congress, 13, 14, 15, 18, 23, 24
Democrat, 18
Department of Corrections

DOC, 67, 69, 70, 71, 73, 74, 77, ⁻78, 79, 80, 81, 82, 83, 84, 85, 90
Department of Defense, 110
Department of Fire and Emergency Medical Services, 90
Department of Housing and Community Development, 90
Department of Human Services, 90
Department of Public Health, 90
District budget, 94
District of Columbia, 1, 2, 3, 5, 6, 8, 9, 10, 13, 15, 16, 18, 19, 20, 21, 23, 24, 25, 26, 27, 28, 30, 31, 32, 33, 34, 35, 36, 37, 40, 43, 44, 45, 46, 47, 48, 49, 50, 51, 52, 54, 55, 56, 57, 58, 60, 62, 63, 64, 65, 66, 67, 68, 69, 70, 71, 73, 74, 75, 76, 77, 78, 79, 80, 81, 82, 83, 84, 85, 86, 89, 90, 91, 93, 94, 95, 96, 98, 99, 100, 101, 106, 107, 109, 110
District of Columbia Bicentennial Commission, 1
District of Columbia College Access Act, 63, 65
District of Columbia Delegate Act, 13, 15, 18, 24
District of Columbia Public Schools DCPS, 49
District of the Columbia Board of Education DCBE, 44
DOC, 67, 68, 69, 70, 71, 72, 76, 78, 80, 82

E

Education, 9, 43, 44, 45, 46, 47, 48, 51, 52, 53, 54, 55, 56, 57, 58, 62, 65, 99, 101, 105, 106
EMA, 108
emergency board of trustees, 49, 52
Emergency Management Agency

EMA, 108

F

Fairfax County, 68, 70, 77, 87
FBOP, 67, 71, 72, 73, 74, 76, 80, 82, 83
Federal Bureau of Prisons
   FBOP, 67, 71, 73, 74, 75, 80, 82, 86
federal education grants, 47
federal monuments, 2
federal prison system, 68, 71, 72, 73, 74, 79, 81, 82, 83
Financial Responsibility and Management Assistance Act, 44, 49, 52, 89, 90
Financial Responsibility and Management Assistance Authority, 25, 49, 52, 62, 89, 90
Ford, 3
Ford's Theater, 3
funding, 5, 46, 48, 52, 70, 72, 78, 97, 102

G

GAO, 70, 106
General Accounting Office, 50, 70
   GAO, 70
general election, 58
general provisions, 93, 94, 95
George Washington, 1, 3, 4, 5, 7, 31, 53
Georgetown, 6, 8, 32
government buildings, 2
growing debt, 90

H

Hawaii, 27, 28
HBCUs, 64

Health, 10, 18, 90, 94, 95, 99, 102, 110
Health Care Benefits Expansion Act, 94, 95, 99
health care expansion program, 95
health insurance expansion, 94, 95
higher education, 63, 64, 79
hijacked aircraft, 4
Historically Black Colleges and Universities
   HBCUs, 64
House Appropriations Committee, 75, 76, 109
House of Representatives, 1, 2, 5, 14, 15, 16, 17, 18, 20, 23, 24, 25, 26, 27, 32, 36, 37, 40
Housing, 90
Human Rights, 105

I

IDEA, 105
illegal drug use, 95
incarceration, 79, 80, 84, 85
incest, 95, 99
income taxation, 24, 25, 38
independence, 5, 15
Individuals with Disabilities Education Act
   IDEA, 105
infrastructure, 3
Infrastructure, 18
inmates, 68, 70, 72, 73, 76, 77, 78, 79, 80, 82, 83
interpretation, 14

J

JFK, 4
John F Kennedy, 4
Johnson, 2, 7, 27
joint resolution, 59, 60, 61
Joint resolution, 60, 61

K

Kennedy, 4, 10, 19, 30
Kennedy Center, 4

L

lead, 3, 53, 89
leadership, 3, 68, 91, 94, 95
LEAs, 50
legislation, 7, 16, 17, 23, 24, 25, 26, 27, 30, 38, 39, 40, 43, 47, 62, 64, 65, 67, 69, 80, 81, 95, 97
legislative control, 95
legislative process, 17
local educational agencies
  LEAs, 50
Lorton Correctional Complex, 67, 68, 69, 72, 74, 77, 78, 81, 84

M

Management Reform Act, 89, 90, 91
Management Restoration Act, 89, 91
Marion Barry, 10, 48
Maryland, 3, 5, 6, 7, 9, 19, 20, 24, 26, 28, 33, 34, 35, 36, 37, 41, 63, 64
Mayor Barry, 11
Mayor Sharon Pratt Dixon, 10
Mayor Walter Washington, 9
Mayor Williams, 91
medical marijuana, 94, 95, 102
Members of Congress, 30, 38, 107
Memorandum of Understanding, 52
memorial flag, 3
Metropolitan Washington Airports Authority, 10
military, 8, 9, 65, 75
mode, 29
Mount Vernon, 3

N

national capital, 5, 6, 32, 33, 35
National Council on Crime and Delinquency
  NCCD, 70, 81
nays, 40
NCCD, 70, 81
needle and syringe exchange programs, 94, 95
needle exchange programs, 94, 95, 102
Northern Marianas Islands, 15

O

operating fund expenditures, 94
operating funds, 94
organization, 39, 44, 55
organizational expedients, 17

P

Pennsylvania, 4, 9, 83
Pentagon, 4
Philadelphia, 1, 2, 4, 7
Philippines, 15
Pierre Charles L'Enfant, 3
Pierre L'Enfant, 1
population, 1, 6, 7, 11, 19, 26, 27, 30, 33, 34, 37, 46, 50, 51, 69, 70, 72, 73, 75, 80, 82
Potomac River, 1, 5, 6, 7, 34
President Bush, 94
President Clinton, 10, 67, 90
President George Washington, 1, 4, 7
President Lincoln, 3
President Lyndon B. Johnson, 2
President Washington, 5
prison system, 67, 68, 70, 71, 73, 76, 77, 79, 81, 82
private institutions, 63
private prison contractor, 71

Index

program, 50, 51, 52, 63, 64, 65, 66, 72, 79, 80, 95, 97, 102
proposals, 14, 56, 68, 71, 83
public education, 43, 44, 48, 49, 50
public laws, 43, 44
Puerto Rico, 15, 16, 21, 23, 24, 39

R

rape, 95, 99
Redskins, 12
reelection, 18, 58
reform candidates, 91
registered voters, 47
repair, 35, 49
Republican, 68
Residency Act, 1, 7
Resolution, 60
resources, 81
response, 107, 108, 109
Rock Creek, 6, 7
Roosevelt, 45, 69

S

Saint Elizabeth's Hospital, 10
scholarships, 63, 64
Scholarships, 63, 64, 65
school expenditures, 50
SEAs, 47
second ballot, 18, 39
security, 4, 70, 74, 78, 79, 80, 83, 94, 109
Senate, 5, 10, 15, 19, 20, 23, 24, 26, 27, 29, 32, 34, 35, 36, 37, 39, 40, 41, 59, 60, 66, 70, 74, 80, 81, 83, 84, 85, 93, 94, 95, 96, 97, 99, 100, 103, 106
Senate Appropriations Committee, 81, 93, 94, 95
September 11, 4, 107, 108, 109
September 11, 2001, 4, 107, 108, 109
social riders, 94, 95

Speaker of the House, 59
special election, 57, 58
St. Elizabeth's Hospital, 10
standing committees, 15, 16, 17
State, 2, 10, 14, 20, 24, 26, 29, 30, 36, 69, 73, 74, 81, 82
state education agencies
SEAs, 47
Supreme Court, 2, 28

T

Taxpayer Relief Act, 67, 72, 74
teacher certification, 47
teenage smoking, 95
territorial government, 8, 13
terrorism, 29, 108
terrorist, 4, 107
terrorists, 4
the Capitol, 2, 3, 73
the Mall, 2
tourism, 12
transportation, 46
Treasury, 38
troops, 3
Tuition Assistance Program, 63, 64, 65
twin towers, 4

U

undergraduate education, 63, 64
United States, iv
United States Constitution, 1, 14, 59
Urban, 18, 45, 46

V

Vice President, 20, 24, 28, 36
Virgin Islands, 15, 16, 21
Virginia, 3, 5, 6, 7, 8, 9, 28, 34, 63, 64, 67, 68, 69, 70, 73, 74, 76, 80, 81, 86, 87

voters, 2, 6, 8, 10, 37, 47, 53, 56, 57, 58
voter-sponsored referendum, 57
voting representation, 10, 19, 20, 24, 25, 26, 27, 28, 29, 30, 31, 35, 37, 38, 39, 94, 95, 97, 102, 103
voting rights, 13, 24, 28, 39
Voting Rights Amendment, 9, 28, 30

W

War, 3, 5
War of 1812, 3

Washington Metropolitan Area Transit Authority, 9, 110
Welfare, 69
White House, 2
Wizards, 12
workers, 108

Y

yeas, 40